Life

INTERRUPTED

Taking Charge After
Everything Has Changed

Michael Parise
M.Div., M.A., C.A.G.S., L.C., C.S.D., C.S.I.T.

Life Interrupted: Taking Charge After Everything Has Changed

Copyright © 2016 by Michael Parise

Michael Parise

michael@parisecoaching.com

ISBN: 978-0-9980956-0-8

Printed in the USA

To Jay T. Whitney
The man who knows and loves me as I am.

Contents

Acknowledgments

I want to express my gratitude first to my spouse, Jay Whitney. His love and support throughout this project has enabled me to explore new corners of being human.

Thanks to my brilliant editors: Denia Fraser and Joanna Guerriere whose cogent suggestions made this book 1000% better than I could have done on my own.

Thanks also to Karen Rowe of *Front Rowe Seat*, my publishing coach who patiently guided me through a daunting process.

I also thank the following people who helped proofread the content and offered me invaluable suggestions of the final iterations of the book: The Rev. Frank Cooper, Martha Cooper, Doug Borowski, Mary Stavro, Michael Sklar, Roberta Lynn Monti, Carol Choban, William McMenimen, and Toby Johnson.

Special thanks to fellow life coaches and kindred spirits, Alla Zollers and Wyokemia Joyner who put me in touch with my possibilities.

Abundant gratitude to my parents, Mike and Mary Parise and my dear friends John and Carmen Donovan, Pamela and Philip Newfell, Mary Ellen Conway, Dr. Jacqueline Stewart, and Dee Morris, whose love and support helped me learn from my experiences, and to Dr. David Mirsky who has enlightened my mind and my soul for forty years.

Testimonies

"The best healers, they say, are the ones who've suffered the wounds themselves. Michael Parise has certainly seen his life interrupted – several times and in different ways. He brings the healer's touch to his book of advice and wisdom. *Life Interrupted* is easy to read, with very little psychological/self-help jargon, and easy to understand and follow, with just enough personal biography to exemplify the message and demonstrate that this former priest and now counselor and life coach knows what he is talking about. The premise of the book is that life can change drastically and the healthy person has to be able to adapt and move on. There is no choice. Parise gives advice and simple exercises to show how to move on."

— Toby Johnson, author of *The Myth of the Great Secret: An Appreciation of Joseph Campbell*

"Michael's book presents the reader with a window into the many interruptions of his multi—faceted life and ways he learned to take charge in spite of change. It is an honest, personal and transparent testimony that change is constant and can be beneficial to anyone's life experiences. It is the result of a unique blend of his pastoral empathy, his personal qualities as a spiritual guide with humility and intuition and his practical wisdom and personal experience as a life coach. In it stumbling blocks of change are transformed into stepping stones toward a life changing direction. It opens one to a present filled with hope and resolve."

— The Reverend Frank M. Cooper, PhD.
Priest in The Episcopal Church, Tampa, Florida

"Major life changes are often frightening, but they can be surprisingly positive. In his new book Michael Parise presents a calm, sensible approach to dealing with and embracing change. Through insightful and sensitive personal observation, along with readily accessible reflections and exercises, Michael guides the reader through the sometimes rough seas of change with encouragement and positivity. This book is for anyone who faces change and would like to welcome it with an open heart and an open mind."

— Michael Sklar, IT Consultant, Red Bank, New Jersey

"Do not read this book if you do not want to be disturbed. Michael led me to reflect upon the pillars holding up my fragile pier. Even though replacing even one of them could cause major chaos, the questions he posed led me to a more solid structure for moving into a better future. It has been said that Jesus came to comfort the afflicted and to afflict the comfortable. Parise's book carries this mission forward."

— Douglas Borowski, Child Support Enforcement Specialist, Worcester, Massachusetts

"Be patient toward all that is unsolved in your heart and try to love the questions themselves like locked rooms and like books that are written in a very foreign tongue. Do not now seek the answers that cannot be given you, because you would not be able to live them. The point is to live everything – live the questions now. Perhaps, you will gradually, without noticing it, live along some distant day into the answer."

— Rainer Maria Rilke, *Letters to a Young Poet*, tr. by M.D. Herter Norton, W.W. Norton & Co., 1934

How to Use This Book

Has your life ever been rudely interrupted? Have you ever experienced major changes that have left you without moorings, and without a sense of direction or purpose? Do you sometimes feel as if you are no longer in charge of your life, or living the life you thought you had? Maybe you are finding yourself wondering what direction is best for you. Are you going with the flow, allowing external circumstances to govern how your days will go? Are you tired of "being there" for others at the expense of your own needs? Have your reached a point where you are finally asking, "What about me?" Then this book is for you. I want to help you re-boot your life and begin again in a way that is connected to, and expresses, the deepest desires of your heart.

Our world is accelerating constantly. We need to find ways to not just catch up, but to intentionally create lives that we enjoy living and that enable us to *thrive* through inevitable change. We need to make our lives our primary projects, so that everything else on our agenda does not just deplete our resources, but adds to our value, wisdom, and contentment.

Many of us currently find ourselves anxious about personal finances, drowning in responsibilities at home and at work, and struggling to catch our breath. The result is that we often feel lonely and isolated. We may also be juggling the emotional dynamics in our families, feel manipulated by faceless bureaucracies, and may be worried about the broad social injustices that oppress our neighbors. We may have experienced successes in our lives and be weary of the price and the struggles which have accompanied those successes. Many of us want to rebel but do not know how. We just want a little love for ourselves.

In the process of this anxiousness, some of us have even lost our self-identity. We have become proficient at judging ourselves and we constantly hear the inner voices of scarcity and defeat. Some of us are so disappointed and disillusioned that we have almost given up waiting for someone to rescue us.

Given up waiting for someone to rescue us? Actually, that is a *good* thing! When we give up waiting for that "knight in shining armor" to sweep down and gather us up on a mighty steed and fly us off into nirvana, then we know we are ready to *change*. This is when we know we are waking up to a new life – a new reality where we can begin to embrace our infinite value. Our hearts are opening up to the truth that we do matter—*each of us*—in a unique and profound way. We can sense a hint of inner peace, renewed hope and the freedom to be fully ourselves. We deserve a pat on the back because we have taken the first step in taking charge of the life we are meant to be living, especially when everything has changed.

This is where this book comes in. I am here as your life coach and spiritual mentor to help you through the process of change – both recognizing when you need to change, and how to move through it to become stronger and more connected to yourself and what matters than ever before.

You can read this book from beginning to end or by skipping around to the chapters that are the most relevant to you. Each chapter is meant to jumpstart an aspect of your life. Taken together, the chapters of this book zero in on transforming the root issues that most influence your personal happiness. Transforming these issues will lead you in the direction of experiencing a meaningful existence in this fleeting world.

I have taken care throughout the book to express life not as a straight line consisting of clearly-defined goals, but as a series of intersecting spirals, or a mosaic made up of thousands of seemingly unrelated and minute moments struggling to come together for the big picture. Each of the pieces and concepts in this book come together, in no particular order, to form the whole, just as in life, certain concepts and insights add elements along your spiritual journey not in a chronological order but in varying degrees at varying times, forming the masterpiece of your life and your journey of transformation.

I have found that with this perspective, most of us can move forward in our own, unique journeys of transformation and transcendence, and can move away from expectations that lead to disappointment and ultimately to resentment, bitterness, and despair and waiting for someone to rescue us. We can become our own rescuer and learn to reset our priorities to include taking care of ourselves first.

I wrote this book because I have discovered the value of interruptions and disruptions in my own life. They used to seem like intrusions into my well-planned strategy for life. Now I welcome them as opportunities to shift gracefully into the mosaic of greater self-awareness and self-confidence. The interruptions and disruptions that were once my enemies have become friends that have helped me to reclaim spiritual responsibility for my relationships, vocation, and life.

So it can be for you as well.

Throughout the course of the book I weave together three intersecting avenues: The first is my own spiritual journey, beginning as a child and continuing through thirty-two years as a parish priest and certified spiritual director in the Roman Catholic Church. The second avenue is my personal life. I share what it has been like being a man with a global vision for the church, wanting it to move forward, and experiencing it as frozen in time. The third, which weaves in and around the other two, is the wisdom and experience that I have gained through struggle and challenge. These qualities have helped me re-boot my life on numerous occasions, most recently when I left the priesthood in 2010 to begin a new chapter as a life coach. I invite you to begin welcoming interruptions in your life and purposely disrupting your thinking and acting in order to take charge of the life you are meant to be living.

In walking these avenues with me I ask that you be critical of your *status quo*. Leave nothing unexamined. Be courageous. Dig deeply and be honest about taking responsibility for choices that you have made, no matter if they have turned out well or disastrous. Examine the events that have shaken up your life. Question your routine spiritual practices and preconceptions around faith and religion. Be open to the serendipity of the Spirit.

Each of the chapters ends with a few reflection questions to help you think, pray, meditate, and contemplate on and about the concepts just presented. Write your responses in a journal. Eventually you will piece together the message that the Universe is placing before you as you read this book.

You will find as you read that I use the terms "God" and "Universe" interchangeably. It is my preference to do so. You may substitute any terms you find helpful to describe your higher power, even if that higher power is simply you. I am writing from the perspective of a life coach and spiritual mentor, not a religious leader. I do not endorse any particular religious or spiritual system.

If you have undergone, or are undergoing, a traumatic change, a shift in relationships, a major disappointment or a sense of being stuck and not moving forward, you may be in new territory and feel the need for support. Reaching for this book is the first step in receiving the support you need and deserve. I am happy to be on this journey with you.

Before we get started, consider the following:

- What do you enjoy about your relationship with your spirituality? What aspects of your spirituality challenge you?
- What is currently causing you the most emotional pain? Think about it for a moment so that you can become eager to change it.
- What brings a vibrant joy to your heart?

Prologue

> "The great thing, if one can, is to stop regarding all the unpleasant things as interruptions of one's 'own,' or 'real' life. The truth is of course that what one calls the interruptions are precisely one's real life – the life God is sending one day by day."
>
> — C.S. Lewis, *The Collected Works of C.S. Lewis*

Though this book is primarily about personal spiritual inquiry and self-help, I believe it is important for you know a bit about me. Everything I have learned about human behavior has been the result of experiencing over six decades of life, half of which as a parish priest, so naturally my background informs my point of view. Much of who I am today as the Life & Spirit Coach has been influenced by my waking up to the fact that Catholic parish ministry no longer fit who I am. I still consider myself a spiritual mentor and intercessor, and always will; but my priesthood was interrupted by my leaving and now resumes in a new format.

Most of us experience interruptions as influences that came straight from God. They are like revelations that unavoidably illumine our lives – true "in your face" moments. Often they ask us to disrupt the *status quo* with an intuitive promise that there is something better ahead.

In June of 2009 my boss, the Archbishop of Boston Cardinal Sèan O'Malley, wanted to see me upon receiving my request for a leave of absence. I was about to interrupt my ministry and disrupt my entire life by leaving the priesthood after 32 years. I arrived at the pastoral center in Braintree feeling overwhelmed by what I was about to do. Taken upstairs to the secured location of Cardinal O'Malley's office I sat down in the waiting area. Fr. Robert Kickham, the Cardinal's private secretary, could not have been nicer.

I was shown to a stiff, modern arm chair and waited. After what seemed a long time Cardinal O'Malley walked in with the Archdiocesan Administrator Fr. Richard Erickson. I shook their hands and sat down, silent, waiting for someone to speak. Eventually Cardinal O'Malley said, "As you know we don't have enough money in the Archdiocese but I'd like to offer you a sabbatical."

I thought about the salaries his top administrators received—ten times that of a pastor—and knew where a lot of the diocesan church's money was going. I just smiled and said, "Thank you, but I've already gotten enough input in my life and don't need more."

It felt odd that in light of my dramatic disruption, at no point did either man ask me why I wanted a leave of absence, what they might do to help me, or whether or not I planned to return to ministry. They seemed strangely detached from any curiosity or concern for a priest who had served for over three decades. I said, "God is leading me to reflect upon my future and I need the time away from ministry to do so."

This elicited sympathetic nods; no other response. The Cardinal stood up signaling an end to the interview, held out his hand, and said, "Let us know if you need anything." During the next year, no one from the Archdiocese called to inquire how I was doing. I received the customary one year of health insurance and nothing else. I had to relinquish any hope of receiving a retirement stipend which I would have gotten only if I had stayed until the age of seventy-five.

Sometimes the decision to interrupt the flow of our lives carries serious consequences. It may even redefine how we have viewed ourselves for decades. It took nearly ten years of reflection and counsel before I was ready to make my disruptive choice. The truth: I was no longer suited to be a parish priest as the church defined the role. I had the education, the credentials, the intellect, the experience, and the knowledge. What was missing was an inner drive to conform to the point of giving up my self-identity. I needed to interrupt what had become merely an unsustainable daily habit.

It is not that I did not try. I had been convinced for a couple of decades that the church's party line—its official teachings on faith, morals, and religious practices—was the way to go. I had even published pamphlets and articles that supported the church's positions. I had embraced the party line as a quilt of many colors carefully held together for millennia by sacred tradition, scripture, and history, creating a cohesive and cogent picture of what heaven on earth could be like.

Yet, for me, there was a disconnect between the ideals of the church's teachings and the men who were in charge of running the organization. Most of the men in the hierarchy

I knew seemed to use the party line not just as a source for their teaching and sermons, but also as something to hide behind. They used it to protect them from expressing opinions or engaging their priests in more than superficial conversation. They allowed themselves to become drawn into mind-numbing administration, meetings, and pastoral visitations without expressing who they were as men.

Eventually I learned to let go of my ideals as I discovered that the party line was somewhat an illusion – a compendium of interesting theological ideas held together by a consistent world view. When I began to pick at any aspect of that world view the whole quilt seemed to fall apart at the seams. And part of that world view was that more than anything else I was supposed to be a gender-neutral shaman *cum* administrative functionary – a middle-management franchiser for the archdiocesan business interests.

I tried every course of action I could think of to disrupt the world in which I was working before making my final decision. My writing was a great outlet for me. My first pamphlet published by *Liguori Publications* in 1985 entitled, "A Catholic Looks at Evangelical Christians," was an attempt to affirm the most important matters of faith that each side embraced. *Liguori* also published three more of my pamphlets: "Evangelization: Spreading the Good News," "The Laity: Called to Build God's Kingdom," and "Are We the One True Church?" These were calls to ordinary Catholics to use their authority in spreading the faith. In my booklet, "Ecumenism: That All May be One," I emphasized the value of dialogue and mutual understanding among Christians.

This literature went into multiple printings and reached over a million people. For several years I was also a featured "Dear Padre" contributor, which appeared in thousands of Catholic weekly parish bulletins. I answered questions, offered advice and explained basic church matters. Among other articles I also published seventeen works on parish ministry in *The Priest* magazine and co-wrote a catechism for *Pauline Books.* With the exception of a few fellow clerics, my writing seemed to have been met with total indifference among the archdiocesan leadership.

The article of which I was proudest was the cover story in the *National Catholic Reporter* in June of 2006, three years after the clergy sex abuse scandal broke out in Boston. In it I wrote about the victimizing not only of those who suffered the actual sexual abuse, but also those who were kept in the dark about how serious a matter it had become, especially the priests who had served so faithfully. For many of the clergy, their being blindsided by the revelations did not just take the wind out of their ministerial sails, it shattered their morale and permanently altered their view of the church institution to which they had committed their lives. (see the *Appendix* for the article). I was one of many who were shocked at the Catholic Church's handling of clergy sexual abuse. By the time revelations of it erupted in Boston in 2002 I felt that much of the good that I had done in the church for the previous twenty-five years had been permanently undone.

This was one of the most significant interruptions in my life that I had to learn to change and grow through. I also had several early interruptions that influenced my journey.

My Early Interruptions

Interruptions can be scary and unsettling, leaving us feeling lost, but they can also come in the form of inspiration or something simply tipping us off in a new direction, motivating us to shift our thinking and being. These kinds of shifts were happening to me incrementally as I let go of becoming a dentist in favor of ministry in the early 1970's.

Sometimes world events will motivate us to make shifts. One of the events that had a huge impact on me in this positive, nudging kind of way was the Second Vatican Council. Hundreds of bishops from all over the world had gathered in Rome to meet for only the second time in one hundred years (1962-65). It was dubbed "Vatican II." The bishops restated many of the Church's doctrinal positions in more modern language. One of their signature concepts was the "priesthood of the baptized," asserting that all the members of the church were equally blessed and important; not just the clergy. This, among other teachings, gave me hope that I might galvanize ordinary Catholics to action that would change the world.

Local changes in our environment, in our neighborhoods, and in our home lives are also motivators for us to move to a different stage in life. For me, this kind of interruption came in the form of a newly established parish near my home that embodied the spirit and teachings of Vatican II, St. Eulalia's in Winchester. The pastor, Monsignor Joe Lyons was the kind of progressive and faith-filled man I wanted to emulate. He along with the parish staff, put "flesh" on the new teachings of Vatican II in the everyday worship and ministries of the parish. The weekly Wednesday night guitar masses felt far removed from the staid and formal worship typical in Catholic parishes. I began to feel a part of a vital and alive church and was happy to interact with adults who did not dismiss me just because I was a teenager.

Spiritual enlightenment also often opens our eyes to a new world. This happened for me during the Catholic Charismatic Renewal. This spiritual renewal movement reintroduced the concept of the gifts or "charisms" of the Holy Spirit that St. Paul cited in his New Testament letters. The renewal was akin to the 1920's Protestant Pentecostal Movement. In 1967 the Catholic version of the movement unfolded at Duquesne University and spread to other Catholic universities and institutions. "Baptism of the Holy Spirit," speaking in tongues, and other ecstatic manifestations were essential to the renewal. Speaking or praying in tongues sounded like gibberish, but was thought to be prayer or prophecy from God. Other gifts that had been described in the New Testament were those of wisdom, knowledge, faith, healing, miracles, prophecy, discernment of spirits, teaching, pastoring, and administration. While the renewal reawakened the mystical presence of God for me, I did not remain long associated with it due to confusion among leaders, cliques among followers, and theological disagreements.

In many cases interruptions and transformation come in the form of relationships and friendships. In my second year at Boston University I met Bonnie Plotner and Dennis Gill as I was leaving the library one day. They invited me to a *Seekers* meeting which met on Sunday evenings at the venerable Evangelical Park Street Church in downtown Boston. The meetings consisted of singing, praying, sharing, and listening to the Reverend Wayne Anderson's practical biblical teachings. Within a couple of years the group had grown to over five hundred members. I found a number of kindred spirits and friends there and learned about a respectful kind of gospel-sharing called "discipleship" which attracted people through friendship and service in imitation of Jesus and his apostles. This motivated me to create such a ministry of discipleship in the Catholic Church.

By 1973 I became convinced I ought to dedicate myself to something in line with a more basic human need than dentistry. Dentistry had been the reason I majored in biology at university, but I was starting to feel that spirituality and faith were at the *core* of basic needs. Even though I questioned letting go of sixteen years of studying science and math, I decided to veer away from dental school and to seek acceptance into St. John's Seminary in Brighton in the spring of 1974.

Becoming a priest was not a popular choice among most Catholic families amidst the sexual revolution of the time. Within a decade after Vatican II a lot of Catholics had become increasingly disillusioned. The church had yet to make the changes they believed the Council had proposed, many of which were in their minds more than in the Council documents. The progressive wing of the American church was getting restless. Priests still could not be married. Divorced and remarried Catholics still could not go to communion. Women still could not be ordained. Sharing worship with other Christians was still impossible. Already, over twenty thousand priests in the United States had shown their dissatisfaction and had left to get married. It was no wonder that my father and friends at church felt I was throwing away my life when I decided to give my life to celibate priesthood.

Yet I considered myself somewhat of a non-conformist and invited the opportunity to do something really different and radical with my life. I thus felt good about bucking the trend and going into a life with which most people were not interested. I was also ready to leave my parents' home and to walk in the footsteps of Jesus.

I soon realized, however that it would take a great deal more than freedom from my parents and evangelical zeal for me to fit into the seminary culture. I had hoped my confreres would be as enthusiastic and motivated by the gospel as I was. Instead I found most of them to be a bit jaded. It may have been due to their being in the system for too long. Some had been in seminaries from high school through college and into graduate school. This sequestering to make them into little monks may have contributed to their playing the system in order to preserve a modicum of personal freedom.

My being a bit non-conformist included factors that I did not dream would be an issue, yet they were. Apparently I was one of the few who had not been part of the typical Boston Catholic ethos. I never went to parochial schools. I had gone to a secular university and studied science. I was Italian-American, grew up in the suburbs, and was friends with Protestants and Jews. I was shocked that a Catholic "ghetto mentality" still existed.

I was also dismayed to encounter a number of snarky cliques that thrived in the seminary environment. Some of these were not just unsociable, but cruel. I eventually found a small number of like-minded men who valued spirituality, prayer, and a desire to share the gospel. I defaulted into a routine of study and meditation as I made the difficult transition from the sciences to philosophy and theology.

This was only the start of interruptions on my journey. As I quickly found out, there were more ahead – and some that left me feeling completely lost.

Being Gay

The greatest disruptions in life have often to do with *self-identity*. We may come to realize, usually in our childhood, that either adults or peers do not seem to be satisfied with the way we present ourselves. How we look or communicate, our interests or hobbies, our mannerisms, our academic or physical abilities, our sexualities...all of these can feel like huge obstacles to socializing and fitting in when others label them as "abnormal." Many children who do not quite "fit in" quietly internalize this attitude and begin to walk the path of self-judgment, wondering, *Just who am I?* or, *Why am I different?*

In my early years I was an innocent, guileless child with no particular understanding or interest in sexual identity. I just knew I was a boy who was creative, artistic, dutiful, and intelligent and who had an ironic and quirky sense of humor. After puberty I spent most of my teenaged years waiting for a moment when I would finally wake up to being attracted to someone, just like the other kids in school seemed to be. I did not have a clue as to how that felt.

The root cause for this was that I had emotionally shut down after being bullied in grade eight. The experience left me wondering what was wrong with me that ordinary kids could not just like me for who I was. This, I believe, led me to turn to God more and led me to develop a constricted world-view and a moralistic, judgmental outlook. I had absolutely no experience in dating; virginity was a safe position to embrace.

Soon after I arrived in the seminary I realized that a number of the seminarians were "out there." The innuendo behind much of their joking and teasing was often sarcastic and biting. A number of the guys were either effeminate in their mannerisms and speech, or blatantly seductive. I freaked out a bit, wondering what I had gotten myself into, yet I was also fascinated. I could not figure out how guys who were committed to celibacy and ministry could also act so silly and sound so hedonistic. I also secretly envied them. I now realize that many of them were just letting off steam.

No one spoke publicly about their sexual orientation, though privately comments and gossip flew about who was in love with whom. My friends and I sometimes shared our stories of sexual struggles among each other. The seminary administration encouraged us to be open with our spiritual directors, who were bound by confidentiality. By the age of twenty-three I was becoming more comfortable with the probability that I was gay, though I still did not know what that felt like. After a serious and sadly, non-physical infatuation with another seminarian at the age of twenty-three, I finally woke up and began to understand the power of my sexuality.

After ordination, my desire to put the church and ministry first kept any new infatuations at a superficial level. So strong was my loyalty to the church and my fear of scandal that I did not experience my first passionate kiss until I was forty-eight. I was fifty-two before I would tell a few of my closest friends about being gay. I regret that I never told my parents.

Conforming to a corporate culture, such as the Catholic Church's highly organized system, can keep many interruptions at bay, including being gay. It is easier to "go along and get along" than to step out on one's own into the unknown. Even when we are doing the right thing at work or at home, if our interior spiritual life—who we are—is not consonant with what we are doing, we are going to feel a sense of discord. It is almost as if the disruption is simply waiting for the right moment to burst out and make itself known. This was true for me as I was beginning to come into my own sexual identity while still in the seminary and why I postponed coming out totally for many decades.

The larger issue I was tackling was being celibate in a world that did not understand nor support it. I become increasingly lonely and isolated, realizing that neither the laity nor the hierarchy could provide the kind of community intimacy that celibacy required as a context for healthy living. Priests were held at arm's length, almost always being called "Father." We were constantly in a role – neither male nor female; we were part of a separate gender altogether. Most of us tried to spiritualize celibacy as a means to be more available, as Jesus was. Instead it usually felt like a convenient law that saved the institution from paying appropriate salaries to support priests and their families, as is the practice in Eastern Orthodox churches.

At the time I felt I had no choice but to follow the time-worn path trod by nearly all priests I knew. I simply kept my sexuality a secret, felt a twinge of shame from self-pleasuring, and compartmentalized my life. Deep within I felt incomplete and disappointed in myself and in the system.

An Exploding Crisis

There are distinct moments when a corporation or country implodes due to corruption, poor management, political intrigue or revolution. In these moments the entire population finds their lives disrupted. They become part of the collateral damage, as did millions of people when they discovered how wide-spread the clergy sexual abuse of children had been for decades.

In 2002 the extent of the abuse of minors by priests of the Archdiocese of Boston came to light through the reporting of the *Boston Phoenix* and the *Boston Globe*. Soon newspaper and television reports revealed this to be a national and international issue. Gloom and grief hung over every one of us wearing a clerical collar. Another disruption to ministry. Another interruption to life.

In the scramble to make sense of it all many bishops made the matter worse by conflating *pedophilia* (adults with pre-pubescent children) and *ephebophilia* (adults with post-pubescent teenagers), with the entirely separate matters of heterosexuality and homosexuality. It did not help that the church's official teachings, against the findings of the medical and psychiatric communities, used the term "intrinsically disordered" to describe homosexual orientation. Many bishops assumed that any inappropriate activity between adults and same-sex underage children and adolescents had to have been perpetrated by homosexual males. It did not matter that, in reality, the preponderance of sexual abuse of children is heterosexual, committed by heterosexual and often married, men and women.

Long before the scandal unfolded I was aware that some priests, both gay and straight, had enjoyed affairs with consenting adults. I was not prepared for the magnitude of the scandal of child sexual abuse in the church. I was overwhelmed as details emerged about the large numbers of victims at the hands of pedophile priests and the manner with which the hierarchy had chosen to deal with the issue for many decades.

Even as a young man without an extensive formal education in psychology, I had read enough and consulted with enough therapists to know of the serious nature of child sexual abuse and of the importance of protecting the victim and sequestering the perpetrator. As the press revealed more and more of the story about accused priests, many of whom had been held up to us as admirable for their loyalty to the church, I felt as if the foundations of my vocation were collapsing. I felt betrayed by the institution that I had trusted as a moral compass and that had expected so much of me.

I soon realized that the church at its highest levels had little practical understanding of human behavioral psychology, sexual dysfunction and criminal activity, despite their employment of experts in those fields.

In reaction, the bishops of the United States met in Dallas to formulate a zero tolerance policy which, thankfully, began to address the matter. Such a policy, however overdue and necessary, was bound to create collateral damage, and it did. Many bishops removed accused priests without due process and in many cases, placed them in a perpetual administrative limbo, even when accusations proved unsubstantiated. It often seemed that the church viewed the problem primarily in terms of its pocketbook and to hell with its priests.

The Catholic Church in the U.S. alone paid out over three billion dollars for court costs, settlements, and therapy for victims. Another casualty was the moral contract between the church's bishops and priests. We could no longer depend on our spiritual shepherds for support.

Disillusion

Double standards in how different people are treated in the same situation invites disruption. Eventually someone is going to blow the whistle and others are going to leave the system behind. I chose the latter.

It had been okay to play by the bishops' rules as long as I could respect and trust them. I discovered that most of them had feet of clay, shunned controversy, were afraid to offer opinions, and relied on their status as protection. They also had two very different sets of rules: the ones supposedly for all priests and the ones for them and their friends among the clergy.

I experienced this double standard many times. The most egregious instance was in 1992 when, after struggling two years with an emotionally limited pastor who had no empathy, I sought help from Cardinal Bernard Law who blithely told me, "Do you know what your trouble is, Michael? You're angry, judgmental, and overly idealistic." That ended that discussion and sent me into an emotional tailspin, wondering if being at all idealistic was worth it.

I wondered what more could possibly be asked of me. This is a common result when we experience interruptions and disruptions that do not seem to make sense at first. Yet interruptions can lead to a new vision for our lives. They stop us in our tracks and cause us to question fundamental values that we once embraced but now are no longer working for us, like my being "overly idealistic." I got tired of allowing myself to feel bad about myself on the inside because of things that were happening on the outside that were out of my control. I discovered through all of these experiences that the one thing I always had control of was *myself*. Disruptions and interruptions can be dramatic enough to shift us so that we hit our "bottom" like a thud and *finally tire of feeling victimized by external influences*. It is then that we can take responsibility for our daily decisions and intentions, listening more intently to our hearts, and less to the habitual thoughts of our mind, leading us in a new, hopeful direction.

FOR REFLECTION:

- What are some major disruptions that have interrupted your life?
- How did you react to them?
- Looking back, how have these disruptions made a positive difference in your life?

Chapter 1

Taking Responsibility

"Most people do not really want freedom, because freedom involves responsibility, and most people are frightened of responsibility."

— Sigmund Freud, *Civilization and Its Discontents*

Often we *need* an interruption to move us to take *fuller responsibility* for our lives. If we do not take responsibility in these moments, we often end up shifting the blame to others or to events beyond our control. Sometimes the interruption comes in the form of a traumatic experience such as the breakdown of a close relationship, the loss of a job or the death of a loved one. These experiences shake us up. My first assignment ended with this kind of trauma.

I had been assigned to an older pastor for over two years. He was a smart man whose frugality and need to control often overtook his common sense. It was always a strain to get money out of him to pay for new ministries or even postage. Then he suddenly retired at the age of seventy-four.

The next pastor was a former seminary instructor who I knew and thought of as a friend. It turned out that he had little use for me, my opinions, or my pastoral programs. Within a year he found an excuse to tell me to leave the parish, saying that I had "angered" a lot of people. I was crestfallen. He had been good at masking his dislike for me. I knew that this black mark on my reputation—not seeing one's first assignment to completion—would follow me to my next assignment. I knew that complaining to the diocese would be of no use since he had many friends in high places.

Eventually I turned the situation around into one of taking fuller responsibility in my life and learning from the experience. Of course I felt angry that someone I had considered a friend misjudged me and that he used his authority in a blatantly arbitrary and disrespectful way. Instead of brooding, however, I took the action of seeking a new assignment with a positive attitude, leaving behind any feelings of being victimized. I focused on what I knew I had to offer and eventually found a parish I fit into. It remains the one assignment for which I have the fondest memories as Associate Pastor.

Can you recall a similar kind of situation in your life where you felt blame, either toward yourself or another? These experiences carry with them much disappointment and anger. It is difficult but possible to view such incidents as opportunities to ask ourselves, rationally, "How was I responsible and what can I learn from this?" "How and why did I attract this into my life?" "What is this teaching me about myself?" It is a win-win situation when you can refrain from blaming and instead seek a deeper understanding of how you are responsible for outcomes in your life. You can change the negative and self-destructive feedback into positives. This can add value to your life as you develop the art of nuance and learn to know where your role begins and ends in a situation that seems at first to have gone bad.

I grew up thinking it was common sense to practice responsible behavior. Many do not absorb this perspective growing up. Those of us who *have* learned about the power of taking responsibility know that it is best taught through word. We tend to learn to become more responsible when someone sits us down and explains the context of our actions, the outcome of them, and the price we pay for being *irresponsible*, such as having to pay a ticket for speeding. The attempt to teach people about personal responsibility is ultimately behind all forms and degrees of punishment, from "time outs" to incarceration. It works with some people, but not all.

Responsibility is most powerfully communicated when its message is "caught" by the "student" observing and experiencing the impact of his or her actions and reactions on others in relationships he or she values.

Responsibility trail-blazers have become inspirations and call forth the best in us. These are the Martin Luther Kings of the world who put their lives on the line and show by example the effectiveness of their causes.

My father was a great model of responsibility. He was a member of the *Warren Pals,* a neighborhood organization that a bunch of local boys, mostly sons of Italian immigrants, created for themselves in East Cambridge, MA. They grew up together during the Great Depression of the 1930's and stayed together as friends and comrades, creating a bowling league that lasted for over sixty years. It was through belonging to groups such as these that many people in the "Greatest Generation" learned to take care of each other, to share what little they had, and to show kindness even to the kids who did not quite fit in. Because of their mutual association in groups such as this one and the example that many in the groups set, most of the children of this generation grew up to became responsible citizens, spouses, and parents, often expressing deep care and concern for others.

This is not to say that my father's generation did not also engage in some blaming. Many held long-standing wounds that they got in childhood after having lost their parents through death, enduring poverty, being forced to quit school and go to work, fighting in horrific wars, and then suffering economically when they returned home. Some also experienced the pain of racial segregation, ethnic and religious prejudice and risky labor strikes. But through all of this, they chose to put aside blame whenever necessary and instead took responsibility to make their families' lives a bit better.

In this chapter I will deal with blaming as a dead end. I will discuss how your personal stories influence your attitudes toward life and relationships. I will also address the issue of self-confidence, performance and value, and how these perspectives affect how well you take responsibility for yourself. I will end with an exercise to help you reframe your stories to become more positive touchstones for your daily experience.

Choosing Responsibility over Blaming

"You think that if you blame, you will then be free of those problems, but blame cements you to your problems."

— Bryant McGill, *Simple Reminders: Inspiration for Living Your Best Life.*

Blaming can feel *so good*...at first! It is a "gotcha" moment – a spontaneous and fleeting expression of aggression. Blaming is a chance to deflect attention away from you. After an event like a divorce, the loss of a job, or the death of a loved one to whom you devoted your time and energy, you may feel a shift from grief to blame in order for you to make sense of your experience.

When events like this happen we are asked to change our entire lives to pivot in a way we did not choose. We may end up framing the situation in terms of black and white, right and wrong, and at fault or innocent. Blaming makes us feel righteous and morally superior. But blaming can also blind us to the part we played in the situation leading up to the incident. And, it is an emotional dead-end. It brings with it an element of shame and of being "defective." It victimizes others and negates our status as honorable human beings. We also give up our ability to have any power in changing our circumstances at all when we point fingers and lay blame.

We can get addicted to blaming whether directed toward others or ourselves. Blaming is an emotion more than a rational decision and we can easily find scapegoats, real or imagined, who always seem available to take the blame. If we do enough blaming, it becomes our subtle go-to solution for almost every problem we encounter, even the ones we ourselves create.

Unlike blaming, taking responsibility usually does not feel that great right away. This is because taking responsibility is not a spontaneous emotion like blaming. It is a deliberate and conscious decision that emanates from your heart and your conscience. As such, it influences you as a positive choice you are making and not simply a reaction.

When you take responsibility for being at least partially involved in the outcome of a situation, you acknowledge what you might have done differently to influence a more beneficial outcome for everyone involved. Perhaps, without beating yourself up, you can see how you may have fallen short, and you may be able to dispassionately, and compassionately, identify how you think others may have as well. When you take responsibility, you seek a mutual dialogue: You consult, listen, discuss, compromise, and seek a solution both you and the other party can agree on, given the circumstances. Blaming short-circuits this process and appeals solely to your pride. Blaming also deflects attention from taking care of yourself—attending to your own needs—and instead has you focus on the shortcomings of others. When you blame, you end up wasting a lot of energy feeling you must change other people, all the while languishing emotionally and spiritually.

Where do we get the tendency to blame? Part of it is human nature and part comes from our religious upbringing. The biblical creation story detailing Adam and Eve's fall from grace in Genesis 1-3 gives us a clue. However useful (or not useful, for that matter) to explain our human dilemma, most religions have used at least a version of "The Fall" to explain human sin. Instead of teaching responsibility, the story actually teaches that the strongest get to do the most blaming. Adam blames Eve. Eve blames the serpent. And God the all-powerful blames the lot of them! And only God gets to punish by driving them out of Eden, shaming their nakedness, forcing them to work, and making women endure painful childbirth. The one with all the power gets to blame and punish. But in reality, the converse is true: If we blame and punish we are more likely to dominate others, which really gives us no power at all.

When we instead take responsibility, we eschew raw power in order to become a spiritual force that is a safe container for the flourishing of goodness, justice, and respect. A healthier perspective for the story from Genesis would be centered on responsibility and each of the people admitting their part in the bigger picture. We humans always have the freedom of choice to do what we want or at least *to take charge of our reactions to situations that are totally out of our control*. It is too easy to blame others for not leading us or for taking us down a road with a disastrous outcome. Yet we are the leaders! We cannot give our power over to others and expect them to read our minds. If each of us took full leadership of our lives without expecting someone else to show us the way, we would be a much happier and fulfilled people. We may not like the ultimate outcome of every decision but at least we know we have acted from our core freedom and values. We can learn from the outcome so that next time we make wiser choices. Otherwise it is too easy to put the responsibility on God to fix our problems and then to blame God if we are not happy with the outcome – and that does not get us very far.

Our Stories

> *"There is no greater agony than bearing an untold story inside you."*
>
> — Maya Angelou, *I Know Why the Caged Bird Sings*

We all have stories about our pasts, our dreams, and our disappointments. Blaming can run amok in our stories if we are not careful. Blaming serves to reinforce our status as victims. How we tell our stories indicates what feelings dominate and influence us.

In addition to blame, our stories can also express other feelings that dominate us, influence us, and leave us victims. For example, "I've just had a molar removed and need a $5000 implant that I can't afford," indicates a feeling of scarcity. "I'm struggling to get into a job that has opened up but my resume is not up to date," indicates procrastination. "I don't know how I'm going to pay my rent because my unemployment insurance is running out," denotes fear. And "I just got a promotion but I hate the woman I have to work with," indicates anger. Even though we think we are casually sharing our lives, in these instances we are actually eliciting sympathy for being helpless.

Stories are rarely what they appear to be at face value. They are almost always freighted with a deeper meaning we are trying to communicate, like a parable. They can change our mood in the telling of them and actually sabotage our contentment if we engage in certain stories enough. They live in our heads and we call them to mind in quiet moments, especially when we are feeling stressed. We blow them out of proportion and permit them to trigger sadness, anger, or fear.

The effect in our bodies is dramatic when we are telling certain stories. It is as if the incident were happening in real time, as far as our nervous and hormonal systems are concerned. Victim-stories trigger unhealthy emotions such as blaming, resentment, or revenge. This incites our flight or fight response generated by our reptilian brain, the *amygdala*. When we are in the midst of retelling a stressful story our blood shifts to the reptilian brain and deprives the cortex, the part of the brain where rational thought originates, of blood. Our breathing becomes shallow, our blood pressure rises, and our *amygdala* calls for a cocktail of hormones such as cortisol, adrenaline, and epinephrine that prepare us for a fight or flight response. When we are in fight or flight, we do not have the ability to think rationally or proactively.

There *is* a side benefit to our negative and stressful stories. Years ago, when gardening at my parents' home, I would accomplish a huge amount of heavy labor – digging, planting, rearranging stonework and so forth. I noticed that while working I often occupied my mind with resentful thoughts: I imagined offenses by acquaintances and betrayals by fellow clergy. While these mental scenarios kept alive a certain amount of victimhood, they also produced a huge amount of physically energizing hormones that gave me the strength to garden for hours. This is one reason we carry negative energy around with us. The feelings produce a temporary chemical high. It is how boxers survive the ring. But, although this is a temporary benefit, negative stories will not give you long-term peace, happiness and fulfillment.

When we call to mind painful experiences we easily exaggerate them, as I had done when I was gardening. This exaggeration justifies our judgment and indignation even if the only audience is ourselves! In this way, long-held emotions such as disappointment, disillusionment, resentment, anxiety, or anger maintain a life of their own in our bodies. Even though the temporary good feeling and energetic charge from these stories might feel good at the time, over the long run, painting ourselves as victims is not worth it. They also help the body to produce destructive stress hormones such as cortisol.

Telling our stories of victimhood is also a way we mask our narcissism and put forth an idealized self-image. We get to be the angry victim upset that we cannot live in a perfect world. Our stories can also subvert love, closing us off from self-care. They can tell others, "Here's why you should not like me." It is as if, when we look at our own lives, we focus only on a narrow interpretation like that of the Adam and Eve story and leave out the many other stories of unconditional love found in the Bible, and in our lives.

Self-confidence

> *"We do not believe in ourselves until someone reveals that deep inside us something is valuable, worth listening to, worthy of our trust, sacred to our touch. Once we believe in ourselves we can risk curiosity, wonder, spontaneous delight or any experience that reveals the human spirit."*

> — E. E. Cummings

Self-confidence makes taking responsibility more palatable and neutralizes blaming. Confidence is not an "extra" that some people automatically have and others have to do without. When it seems as though we lack self-confidence, it is only because we have to grow into it gradually through every new experience we encounter, especially when changes occur in our lives.

I had graduated from high school with high honors – thirteenth in a class of six hundred. So when I started classes at Boston University in 1970 I thought I was in excellent shape academically. Within the first week of chemistry and biology, my confidence evaporated. My peers seemed to be much better prepared than I was. I much later realized that the reason I was no longer doing as well was because I was not enjoying the pre-dental program course requisites I was taking. I had actually found my passion in my elective courses, I just did not know it at the time. I had never felt more alive than when I was analyzing the writings of Saint Paul or pouring over Janson's monumental *History of Art*. But I did not have the confidence at that time to switch my course of studies altogether. I felt I had to fulfill the commitment I had begun. And the lack of passion for the program I was in, showed.

Self-confidence is the indefinable quality of fearlessly taking full responsibility for living out our passion in life. It is knowing and believing that we have something important and unique to offer the world. It develops gradually as we make daily choices to adopt positive intentions and a promise to carry them through.

Self-confidence does not arrive through a one-time decision to be confident, any more than we can decide to be an authentic hero. Circumstances align and we permit ourselves to go along with them. It is a mood we project wherever we go.

Performance and Value

Your self-confidence will grow as you learn to divorce performance from value; said another way, as you learn to separate what you do from *who you are*. I recall many instances, especially during the week before Easter, when we clergy would plan for a series of complicated services for Holy Thursday, Good Friday, and the Easter Vigil. I was usually in charge of making sure the "supporting cast" of cantors, servers, lectors, and communion ministers knew what they were doing and when. All it took was one person making the wrong move to throw everyone else off. Or so I thought. I had been valuing myself by my performance, meaning, if something went wrong, it meant *I* was wrong – that I had let down the parish and disappointed everyone including myself. I soon learned the limits of thinking this way.

Many of us are more motivated by doing well—or by trying not to disappoint—rather than by a strong sense of who we are and keeping a positive self-regard no matter what happens. When we cease linking performance with personal value we give ourselves the permission to take fuller responsibility for loving ourselves. When we celebrate our infinite value and not let it be dependent on how well we did our job, then there is no need to fulfill anyone else's expectations. We can feel whole and complete as we are.

The performance/value game also touches our personal relationships. Have you ever used your partner or spouse as a sounding board for your self-worth? For example: "Did you notice the work I just did around the house?" Or sometimes our thoughts betray insecurities, for example: "If he loved me enough he'd have picked up his dirty clothes," "I wonder if I made a mistake marrying a woman who just doesn't communicate," or, "I sometimes wish I had another set of kids." Some of thoughts are normal if they are fleeting, but repeated often enough, they become judgments that indicate how much value we place in ourselves or others and become self-fulfilling prophecies. They create a mood that is a dead end in personal relationships, sabotage communication and positive attitudes, and tear down our sense of self-worth.

Identifying and Reframing Stories

"It's like everyone tells a story about themselves inside their own head. Always. All the time. That story makes you what you are. We build ourselves out of that story."

— Patrick Rothfuss, *The Name of the Wind*

The stories you tell most about yourself are the stories that most readily come to mind, and are those by which you define your life and seek attention. They may be stories filled with contentment and victory over struggles. Or, they may be victim stories told to garner sympathy. Here is an exercise to help you identify the stories you tell most about yourself – the stories that you use to define who you are. Once you have identified them you will be able more consciously to choose which ones you would like to be your default stories—which ones you *want* to define who you are—and which ones you want to let go of.

Five Steps to Identifying and Reframing Your Stories.

First, on one page of your journal, begin to write down the stories of your life that you recall and enjoy telling. These may be stories you tell as remembrances or as ways to re-mind people of the difficulties you have had in life. All of them have value and all have taught you something. Some come from your mind and some from your heart. Many may have unresolved emotions attached to them. They may make you feel happy or sad, full of joy or stress, or elated or re-traumatized. There is no need for details – just jot down the general outline of each story, one per line. Here are some examples:

> *"The waiter forgot to put in our order at our anniversary dinner; we had to leave to get a bite to eat at a fast food joint."*

> *"I married a woman who has helped me become less selfish."*

> *"My parents made me feel whole, complete, and loved after my brain tumor."*

> *"I received a raise but it was not as much as I expected."*

> *"My brother bullied me for years and my parents didn't do anything to help me."*

> *"My father kept me from marrying the boy I loved."*

> *"My mother kicked me out of the house when I came out to her as a transgender male."*

"My boss wouldn't listen to my ideas of how I could use my skills to build the business."

Next, put a single check mark (✔) beside the stories that you know are important for you to remember – the stories that motivate you to grow and move forward in your life. These are stories that have now been mostly resolved, even if you first experienced them as unpleasant events. They no longer carry an emotional overload. They lead you to feel hopeful.

Third, put a double check mark (✔✔) next to the stories that are important to remember but that no longer serve a purpose. They hold you back, creating unnecessary defensiveness or resentments. They continue to trigger feelings of conflict. They give you a jolt of energy when you tell them but in reality they emphasize your victimhood rather than your completeness and competency.

Fourth, copy the stories with the single check mark onto a separate page. These are your "Heart Stories." They engender positive feelings of self-worth and love. They affirm your struggles and your successes. Recall one or two of them every day to remind you of the value and purpose of your life.

Fifth, copy the stories with the double check mark onto a separate piece of paper. These are you "Mind Stories." They are important to recall and need continued resolution, but do not need to define your life anymore. They no longer need to take up space in your imagination. You do not have to tell them over and over again. Promise yourself to that you will avoid telling yourself these stories. Seal this piece of paper in an envelope, or if you are writing on a computer, sequester this file in a personal folder you do not often open. If you find yourself defaulting into a Mind Story, take out your Heart Story list and reflect upon one or two of them instead. In this way you can retrain your mind to listen more to the truths you know about your value in your heart.

FOR REFLECTION:

- What areas of your life are currently the most challenging for you to take responsibility for?
- If you were to tell a new story about your life, what would it be?
- What motivates your sense of fairness, love, justice, generosity, loyalty and kindness?
- What are your sources of self-confidence?

Chapter 2

Your Powerful Intuition

"I believe in intuitions and inspirations...I sometimes FEEL that I am right. I do not KNOW that I am."

— Albert Einstein

"When you reach the end of what you should know, you will be at the beginning of what you should sense."

— Kahlil Gibran, *Sand and Foam*

These men were geniuses in different fields: Einstein, a physicist, gave us nuclear fission and Gibran, a spiritualist, wrote poetry that continues to change lives. Yet, both men approached life through *intuition*.

When changes happen—when our life shifts like an earthquake and interruptions give way to deeper disruptions—we have a responsibility to listen to our hearts and discover what is occurring, not just outside of us, but deep within us. Our minds, filled with rational thoughts, analyses and empirical evidence, do not suffice at times like this. Our instincts are too wedded to our primitive brains to discern through any other means. It is in these moments that our hearts—where our intuition echoes—best inform us.

Intuition is vital for protecting our personal boundaries. When we sense something is not quite right at work or at home, we can trust our intuition. We should see flashing yellow lights in our mind's eye saying, "Caution!"

When I was fifteen years old I worked in a large retail greenhouse. One day my manager told a group of us to do a job that would be under the leadership of one of the other teenagers. I met this young man for the first time that day and I had a gut feeling he was not to be trusted. During the job he horsed around and left the real work to the rest of us. When we were finished, he decided to take a cigarette break just as the owner of the complex walked in. The owner was livid and told all of us to go home. My gut told me to speak up, so I said, "Mr. Mahoney, I was just waiting to be told what we were supposed to do next." He smiled and told me to see my boss and stay at work. I really needed that dollar an hour! I learned that day to listen to my intuition and act on its promptings to protect my interests.

Through your intuition you can sense the emotional landscape of your environment, how you are interacting non-verbally with those around you, and what your deepest desires are telling you about the next step you ought to take. Intuition opens up a whole way of knowing the means by which you can understand something immediately, without the need for conscious reasoning. It is also at the heart of prayer and contemplation.

Intuition is really not magical, though in our technological culture we are led to believe it is. Hunches and gut feelings that emanate from our intuition are rooted in our past experiences and knowledge. Intuition enables us to begin analyzing our present situation amidst often confusing feelings so that we can sort out the best next step to take.

Our intuition "calls" to us through a sensation in the body. It often shows up as a tightness or fluttering in the chest or in the abdomen. This feeling alerts us to take a breath—a pause—that gets us ready for imminent new information. Those with a highly-developed intuition such as effective life coaches, counselors, therapists and psychics depend on this "sixth sense" as a portal into the lives of their clients, helping them to uncover the truth that has always been in their hearts.

Physicists tell us that all matter is a form of energy vibrating at different frequencies. That energy comprises 98% of the universe and matter only 2%. We are thus interconnected in one universal intuitive network. Many people believe this network also is a matrix of energy that supports the spiritual consciousness of all beings. The essence of this universal consciousness, which some conceive of as heaven, is the same energy that activates our intuition.

In this chapter I will talk about the types of intuition and the many ways intuition speaks to us. Then I will discuss the discerning of values, especially our *core values* which are pivots around which our intuition gives us messages and our minds make decisions. I will also look explain how following our intuition brings us ultimate contentment.

Types of Intuition

Intuition comes in many "flavors," and depending on our personalities and interests, one or more of the flavors will influence us at any given moment. The following list is not an exhaustive list. Using each of the different types of intuition, practicing them and appreciating them can help us become more emotionally intelligent and more aware of the spiritual messages we are receiving on a daily basis. *Spiritual intuition* may reveal itself to us in a huge event or, more often, in a tiny whisper deep inside our souls. We become more and more able to hear this voice in prayer or meditation as we mature in our self-awareness and in our relationship with higher spiritual powers. The messages we receive may nudge us toward a more fervent religious experience or toward the next good thing in store for us in our lives. Or, they may ask us to deal more honestly and directly with a relationship. The universe around us is constantly gifting us with useful and important information; all there is to do is simply quiet down enough to hear it and learn to receive these messages through our spiritual intuition.

Cognitive intuition especially shows up in intellectual and analytical people. They are able to easily gather information about another person's needs and can come up with a good solution when one's needed in a particular situation. They remain calm and are not taken in by strong emotions. Their logic and sensible questions and responses make them great life coaches and counselors. Your cognitive intuition will show up for you in your thought and analytical patterns and abilities.

Feeling intuition is centered around our hearts and souls and the sensations in our bodies. Our hearts can sense feelings instantaneously and more readily than any other part of our bodies. Those who feel from the heart have an extraordinary degree of empathy and compassion. They may, however, also struggle with codependence as their compassion sometimes overrides their common sense and can get in the way of having appropriate personal boundaries.

Gut intuition is often considered the most common. It is a sensation that seems to emanate from the pit of our stomachs. Gut intuition helps us to read people's personalities and characters. It warns us of danger and tells us when we are emotionally in a great place. It identifies contentment and it helps us identify the "sinking feeling" when it comes up so that we can look at the situation through our mind's eyes and formulate a beneficial plan of action.

Tactile intuition is extremely common, though under-appreciated in our fast-paced world. The palms of our hands and soles of our feet are filled with nerve centers that link to the rest of our bodies. Through them we sense the energy of others even from a distance. Have you ever felt a shudder up and down your spine when someone walks into your office? You sense it is someone very important...and she turns out to be the company president? People who are tactile intuitives tend to excel in hands-on activities like massage, pottery making, carpentry, surgery, painting, gardening, writing, and cooking. They use their touch to heal and communicate and receive a huge amount of information from others through their hands.

Intuition may emerge initially as a sensation in the body, but it needs to then be interpreted and tested and determined to be an accurate assessment of a situation. Opinions, thoughts, beliefs, and scientifically proven facts each get analyzed in different segments of our minds and also need to be taken into consideration. Our feelings, while residing in our hearts, also need to be filtered through our cognitive understanding. It is important to acknowledge here that empirical and rational ideas that have led to scientific breakthroughs often began their journey of discovery as intuitive hunches originating in the heart.

Intuition and Values

Values are beliefs about ourselves, others, our career, our environment, and our spirituality that guide us each day in nearly every decision we make. Our values are what we are willing to live and die for. They govern every aspect of our lives, from what we are willing to pay for toothpaste, to the life-partner we choose. The main purpose of intuition is to create a continuous loop of information that enables us to check in with our values and determine whether or not they are being respected in a given circumstance.

Values might include external matters such as food, comfort, shelter, or financial security. They also include intangibles such as faith, intimacy, friendship, spirituality, collaborative work, and mutual respect. They factor into everything we say and do. Through our intuition, our values inform our conscience as to the next appropriate word or action. They act as attitude-adjusters so that our responses to challenges come from our *personal integrity* and not simply from our emotions.

We begin for formulate our most important values during adolescence. This is why teens constantly question adults – they are discerning which of their family's values fit into their own personal lives. This is a time of experimentation, testing, and risk-taking, and arguing usually follows. As we grow up we also experience the consequences of poor judgment and decisions that are not in line with our own personal values and we find out what happens when we make choices that clash with parental or societal values.

As adults, we continue the process of discerning our values and we throw out or reform those that no longer work in our best interests or in the interests of our community. It is always a good idea to question values one by one and to discover if they really make sense or if they are competing with a seemingly opposing value. To do this work of discernment, we need a strong intuition and deep spirituality that roots our values and beliefs in *who we are in this moment* and not just who we think we ought to be based on external influences such as parental expectations, religious formulae, or government dictates.

We need courage in this process of values discernment. Valuing integrity, for example, may cause us to disrupt our routines, relationships, or working conditions in a dramatic way. At the same time, valuing prudence may mean postponing such action until the time and circumstances are in our favor.

Usually one or two core values govern and motivate all of the other values you hold. These foundational values originate from *within* you and cannot be imposed on you by formal religion, social ethos, or political platforms. Your core values manifest and reveal themselves as you experience life and define your character. They help you make judgments about what is ultimately important to you and guide you in how you can best project yourself in the world.

Once you identify your core values, you are apt to come into conflict with those who either do not respect them or who have core values that are not in harmony with yours. Unfortunately we have seen in history how often this sort of value clash has led to wars between tribes and nations. Such conflicts in values are at the heart of accusations of police brutality, LGBTQ rights, divorce actions, and the legalization of medical marijuana, to name a few. In cases like these, respectful and dignified dialogue becomes an option once the parties involved let go of their expectations and are willing, dispassionately, to at least listen to the other's point of view. It is an art to be able to stand in your core values and listen to those of another without making judgments, feeling threatened, or wanting to reform them.

Many of us recognize conflicts like this at work, where personal relationships are not supposed to play a huge role and where managers are supposed to apply objective standards across the organization. Yet clashing values are at the heart of productivity, advancement, hiring and dismissals. When we become aware of such a clash, we may need to slow down the emotions that well up in our hearts and ask our intuition, *To what am I reacting exactly and why?*

Once you know your emotional triggers, you are able to view value conflicts less passionately and open avenues for reasonable dialogue. You are also then able to calmly make plans for your future when the other parties involved in the situation are not yet able to recognize the need to resolve clashes in values with those around them.

Practicing using your intuition in daily interactions at home can exercise your "honesty muscle," keeping you on the path of open, direct communication, and enabling you to practice integrating your authentic feelings with the love that is at the heart of your family relationships. Such candor and honesty centers you and leads you to a freedom of Spirit that itself becomes a core value and nurtures love. With practice we learn to live a full and rich life, on purpose.

Intuition and Contentment

Listening to your intuition which serves your values automatically supports your well-being and contentment. Every night while you sleep your body literally remakes itself using the food, air and exercise you fed it during the day. Yet it is not just about your body; in your waking hours you also ingest unseen and intangible elements that either feed your Spirit and your level of contentment, or that diminish you and your humanity and cause negativity or manufactured stress.

If you wish to feel the contentment that is rooted in and comes from following your intuition, then self-talk is a great way to start. Try this:

Three Steps to Intuitive Peace

First, consciously focus on and slow down your breathing. Breathe in through your nose for four heartbeats, hold for two and release through your mouth for four beats. Repeat several times until you feel your body relax and are able to focus on the sound of your breathing without distraction.

Second, place the palm of your right hand on your heart. Close your eyes or focus your sight just in front of you. Feel the warmth from your hand/heart connection. Feel it as if it is a tender hug. Keep breathing slowly and rhythmically.

Next, sense your heartbeat and the energy field emanating from your heart. Listen to your quietest inner voice. Look for messages such as:

"All will be well."

"You are enough."

"I love you."

"There is nothing to fear."

"I will never leave you."

"You are wonderful just as you are."

"I'm so grateful for you."

"You are powerful and beautiful."

Spend some time like this each day. Allow your intuitive voice to deliver the sense of well-being you crave. Express gratitude for your intuitive self in whatever way feels comforting.

High Sensitivity and Intuition

"Highly sensitive people are too often perceived as weaklings or damaged goods. To feel intensely is not a symptom of weakness, it is the trademark of the truly alive and compassionate. It is not the empath who is broken, it is society that has become dysfunctional and emotionally disabled. There is no shame in expressing your authentic feelings. Those who are at times described as being a 'hot mess' or having 'too many issues' are the very fabric of what keeps

the dream alive for a more caring, humane world.
Never be ashamed to let your tears shine a light in
this world."

— Anthon St Maarten, author of *Divine Living:*
The Essential Guide To Your True Destiny

People with a highly developed intuition may also be part of the fifteen to twenty-percent of the population also wired to be highly sensitive. Psychologist Dr. Elaine Aron, who authored, *The Highly Sensitive Person* (Three Rivers Press, NY, 1996), has written the most about highly sensitive children and adults. She tells us that high sensitivity is a personality trait—not a neurosis—that carries with it particular characteristics often not understood by the majority of the "hearty" population. Those who are not highly sensitive are likely to have someone in their family or circle of friends/colleagues who is.

Highly sensitive persons (HSP's) find their trait to be a challenge and a gift. With it they can often sense the feelings of others and read their moods. HSP's are often overwhelmed by the sensory input of their environment. They notice details many others miss and take in large amounts of information almost instantaneously. Their empathy can be so strong at times, and affect them so deeply, that they may mask it with a demeanor of indifference or ennui. Highly sensitive people vary in the kinds and degrees of traits they possess but they all exhibit traits within this same constellation of characteristics.

Feeling isolated is a trait that often shows up in highly sensitive children at an early age. They often appear to be antisocial and do not mix easily with other their peers. Nor do they enjoy team games, sports or playing rough. They may burst into tearful frustration for no apparent reason. Many are bullied mercilessly by peers. They also often have fantastic insights into spiritual matters.

Highly sensitive adults do not tolerate visual chaos, often worry a great deal about details, and can appear moody to others. They tend to work well by themselves, are terribly reliable, and are intelligent high-achievers. They are the ones at parties who you will see locked in deep conversation with one individual and ignoring the buzz around them. They shun small talk and tend to attract people looking for advice with their highly intuitive listening power. Some have an almost psychic ability to read people's lives. They often live in their minds and often have a more difficult time than most shaking off unpleasant experiences.

High sensitivity knows no gender preference. Men, especially in Anglo-Saxon countries, are expected to be tough, independent guys, impervious to almost all emotions except anger, jealousy, and aggression. Highly sensitive men generally do not fall into this stereotype. They are often labeled by peers as effeminate, gay, or not "man enough."

Highly sensitive women in our culture are more likely to be accepted if they appear in control of their emotions. When they do exhibit strong feelings in the workplace, they pay an even higher price than men, being labeled as hysterical, neurotic, moody, angry, or threatening.

Working with the highly sensitive sometimes takes patience. Highly sensitive people may take longer times than others to make decisions and can become particularly upset if they think they made the wrong one. The majority are introverts and need to be alone to recharge their emotional batteries. Yet a large percentage of the highly sensitive are true extroverts and recharge by being social. To understand the difference between introversion and high sensitivity I recommend Susan Cain's, *Quiet* (Random House, 2013). For more information about highly sensitive men and women and to take a simple self-test visit Elaine Aron's site at http://hsperson.com.

Many gay men will speak of feeling as if they did not fit into society as children and young adults. This was true for me as well. My theory, however, is that there is a higher percentage of HSP's in the gay population than among straight men. Their feelings of isolation may have originated more in their experience of being highly sensitive than in being gay.

As an HSP learns to integrate their high sensitivity, they will develop a streak of independence as they learn to hold to their emotional boundaries and not give too much of themselves to others too readily. Once they have come to understand the power of their trait and how best to use their qualities of empathy and intuition, they will not feel as isolated. They will project inner strength and resilience and develop greater confidence in who they are.

Saboteurs

Wherever you fall on the scale of sensitivity, you have inner *saboteurs*, or voices that conspire to rob you of your confidence. The strongest inner saboteur for many of us is the "Judge." The Judge questions our value and self-respect, our motives and performance, and whether or not we are likeable.

We can counteract the effects of the Judge by listening more carefully to our inner "Sage," the voice of wisdom, comfort, understanding, appreciation, curiosity, self-management, learning, intuition, and listening. The voice of the Sage reminds us of the non-negotiables on which we have committed ourselves to base our lives. Empathy and our intuition help us to listen to this voice of compassion.

Often it is when someone violates our boundaries that we are jolted into reality. In cases like this, we feel disrespected as if someone has taken advantage of our good nature, our dignity, or broken our trust.

Following your inner Sage leads you to a more functional, happier life where you are gentle with yourself, focused on what really matters, and willing to accept change. It is important to build up your Sage because that voice will help you maintain your emotional boundaries.

We all have areas in which our emotional boundaries need shoring up – areas where we are particularly vulnerable to being disrespected. Our desire to be liked, to live and let live, or to give the other person the benefit of the doubt can set us up to have our emotional boundaries violated. We may need to be more conscious of what kinds of personal energy we want to let into our lives, the intensity with which we want to initiate relationships, the degree of trust and self-disclosure we are comfortable granting in those relationships, and our overall expectations of others both personally and professionally.

Some people actually emit an energy that is toxic to our emotional and spiritual lives and those of us who are highly sensitive or who tend to be "helpers" are particularly attracted to these kinds of people. I am referring here to narcissists. These are usually fascinating, outgoing individuals who automatically consume other people's time and attention. They are attracted to empathic listeners who are willing to entertain their incessant self-centeredness. The same kind of toxic energy can come from some victims of abuse or trauma who have yet to receive appropriate protocols for healing. Those who hate being alone for a host of reasons will also dominate sympathetic souls. Before we know it, these kinds of encounters can overwhelm us, even if we ignore it out of a misplaced feeling of responsibility or guilt. Especially when these kinds of relationships involve close family members, we need to step back before being helpful and take stock of how best to care for ourselves first so we do not get depleted.

Filtering your contact with certain personalities and learning to say "no" to toxic encounters are first steps in strengthening emotional boundaries. There is nothing immoral or unethical about avoiding situations or people who you know will trigger your desire to run the other way. You just have to admit to yourself that it is okay to feel that way, get rid of any guilt around your decision and take the best course of action for yourself. Express yourself through honest discussion and unambiguous statements of how you feel violated or misused. You may have to accept the fact that the other will not understand or may over-react or even reject you. Careful not to take the bait – you might also need to avoid responding to phone calls, texts, or emails.

Areas where we need particularly strong boundaries are in dealing with the mentally ill, especially if they are not using their prescribed medication, and in relationships where there is active substance abuse, domestic violence, sexual abuse, or emotional abuse. We have to learn to be firm about protecting our self-interests even to the point of cutting off communication rather than enabling the other. Self-care also means getting professional support and not being afraid to ask for help with managing these relationships and our boundaries, if we need it.

Stress and Trauma

Our ability to hear our intuition and our emotional boundaries can be skewed by stress and trauma because stress immediately places us on a defensive footing. Some stressful situations are actually healthy, propelling us into productive activity. For example exercise, hard work, deep thought, and even hobbies all produce positive stresses in the body and mind that release pleasant hormones into the blood and can relieve anxiety, fear, and depression.

But much stress is the product of an overly fast-paced society that makes us feel crazy and overwhelmed. The emotions associated with negative stress and emotional traumas become imprinted in our bodies and minds. We "remember" these experiences through having repeated physical sensations in our chests, muscles, and guts which get incited by hormones that are released when we think of the event or are in another stressful event that we perceive to be similar to the first.

Trauma such as physical or sexual abuse, emotional battery, the experience of armed conflict, natural disasters, and major injuries can permanently change our brain chemistry. These events shake our self-identity and reduce our defenses to further trauma. Trauma ends up defining us. We grit our teeth and move as if sleepwalking as we try to shake the effects that the trauma has had on our nervous systems. Sometimes denial of how we really feel, hyper-vigilance against any recurrence, hyper-sensitivity to offenses, and seething resentment, all natural responses to trauma, actually *reinforce* its effects on us. During the process of recovering from trauma and trying our best to deal with it, we can lose sight of our emotional boundaries and may need professional therapy to rebuild our lives and help us deal with the symptoms of trauma that get repeatedly played out in our bodies and Spirits.

Stress is much more common than trauma – so common that we have built our reactions to stress into our emotional boundaries as a normal part of our lives. Many who have common stressors in their lives such as in teaching, speaking in front of groups, changing jobs, getting along with coworkers or family, or relocating have responded well to *Somatic Intuitive Training* ™, which is an emotional intelligence protocol that can reduce stress and help in trauma recovery. This protocol is based on intuition and memory. During the process the client names a feeling that comes up, identifies where it shows up in the body as a sensation and to what degree, and then recalls an older memory that brought up similar feelings and physical sensations for them. The protocol enables the client to rework the emotions around the older memory and replace the previous, negative sensations in the body with new ones of peace and confidence. By becoming more and more aware of the connection between their body and their feelings whenever a stressor shows up and practicing these new and relaxing interpretations and sensations, clients gradually rewrite their emotional history.

Your intuition is the starting point for all healing. It discerns and strengthens your values and promotes contentment and peace in a stress-filled world. As you become aware of how sensitive you are and can be, practice setting healthy boundaries and learn to listen to the connection between your feelings and your body, you strengthen your emotional boundaries and progress toward fuller integration of body, mind, and spirit. Developing and listening to your intuition is the key to living fully without apology or explanation.

FOR REFLECTION:

- What are the three values you hold highest?
- How do your values make you stronger in what you believe is your purpose in life?
- When is your intuition the strongest? In what circumstances do you need to listen to it more?
- After taking Elaine Aron's self-test at http://hsperson.com, what did you discover about your level of sensitivity?
- Which of your emotional boundaries need strengthening?

Chapter 3

The First Imperative

"The irony is that if we make every imperative into a command to believe the gospel more fully, we turn the gospel into one more thing we have to get right, and faith becomes the one thing we need to be better at."

— Kevin DeYoung, *The Hole in Our Holiness: Filling the Gap between Gospel Passion and the Pursuit of Godliness*

First imperatives are the root presuppositions on which we base our lives. They find their ultimate source in our core values, whether these core values come from freedom or fear. Unlike core values which are firm and unchanging, however, they are fluid; they shift according to the circumstances in which we find ourselves, especially when we are in new situations. They are often formed as a result of lessons we have learned the hard way or through being wounded emotionally, taken advantage of, or hurt by our own lack of awareness. They also get formed as a result of major changes in our life like status, career, and relationship changes. First imperatives become our prime movers and form the basis of how we show up in the world. They directly inform the personal choices we make that keep us safe in the present, shape our future, and free us from unnecessary external obligations.

First imperatives also define the limits of our personal boundaries, for example: "If she does not get professional help for her addiction, I'm going to ask for a legal separation." Imperatives are much stronger than requests and are akin to intentions. They are designed to focus us, to limit our choices, and to steer us toward actions that we firmly believe will enhance our lives, until we learn something new and change them, for example: "When I get through these cancer treatments I'm going on a long vacation to visit at least five national parks."

We also create first imperatives that support our lifestyle. These often get formulated following stressful experiences, for example: "After being mugged I will never again walk through the park at night," or, "I'm tired of living a lie; tomorrow I'm telling my family that I'm gay." For more serious traumas, such as abuse, bullying, or domestic violence we form first imperatives for the long-term that we use to remind us never again to return to the past, for example: "After management humiliated me in public for problems they created I am finding a new job and never again setting foot in that company," or, "His PTSD is getting so out of hand that I'm going to ask that he get hospitalized."

First imperatives can be very powerful as they command many facets of our lives and strongly influence the choices we make, the friends we choose, the careers we consider, and even the emotions we will entertain. A healthy first imperative can be a personal bias toward a generous, free and productive life of service and love toward others while still taking care of our own needs. An unhealthy one can shut us down emotionally, close us off relationally, and foster feelings of paranoia, resentment, and victimhood.

We are very familiar with the concept of an imperative, even though we might not call it that. People who are responsible for others such as law enforcement personnel, military leaders, parents, and teachers learn to use an imperative as a means of controlling, commanding, and protecting the people for whom they are responsible. Every family also has a "first imperative." Normally it addresses the primacy of the parents' relationship and the care of and nurturing of the children. Governments usually have a first imperative: to keep the citizens of their nation safe and secure and to provide necessary services to help them live in peace and freedom. Companies have varying first imperatives. Some focus on providing goods and services for customers and having happy employees and others focus on ensuring productivity and profits for stockholders.

As you take new responsibility for your life and begin to sense through your intuition the next good step you ought to take, you will likely find you will want to let go of external influences that no longer serve you. As you learn to trust your intuition more and more, you can begin to respect how you are wired emotionally and realize that *you* come first – not all of those items on your "must do" list that pile up in the course of your day or that flow

73

out of habit, family tradition, work, or religion. More and more, you will likely find yourself taking a moment first to assess each command, rule, or regulation to see if you can find a value in each that you can embrace and that is important to you.

You will find that if you cannot find a resonant value in external imperatives, you may need to reframe the command in question, make it your own more consciously, or reject it altogether and replace it with a new imperative that works for you. Begin to ask yourself, "In what way does this absolute command give me life and in what way does it rob me of contentment and peace?"

In this chapter I want you to think about first imperatives that can change your life, beginning with loving yourself. As you deepen your self-love you will then begin to let go of the need to win or lose as the only choices in life. Finally I will address embarking on new beginnings.

Loving Ourselves

Loving ourselves ought to be a large part of our primary imperatives. Even though we may not have received adequate or healthy parenting growing up, we can learn to take care of ourselves so that we parent the "inner child" who still lives in our souls. Such a first imperative would support a prejudiced concern for our personal needs to be cared for *before* we reach out to assist others. This balance in attitude is necessary, even though it sounds selfish at first. We simply have to keep our own emotional resources in mind before we spend our energy on or for others.

Religion itself can provide a number of ready-made first imperatives, for example: "Love God and your neighbor," "Judge not unless you be judged," and "Only those without sin may cast the first stone." Religious people are motivated to serve, yet sometimes this service is tainted by proselytizing. Some religious persons have a "need to be needed" or to prove to God that they are worthy of personal righteousness. If service does not flow from freedom of will, it is slavery. It is important for you to examine the religious imperatives you have adopted as your own.

Many who have no connection with religion may have a first imperative that says, "If I do the right thing I should be able to get something back." This notion has deep cultural roots. It comes from a business model and has infiltrated almost everything we do socially, culturally, commercially, and politically. This *quid pro quo* attitude is the antithesis of altruism and carries with it little need for personal sacrifice for the common good. What if we reframed it to, "If I do the right thing I may receive good in return, eventually and unexpectedly?"

Creating your first imperative is not a time for negative self-judgment, comparisons with paragons of altruistic virtue such as Mother Theresa, or envy of those who seem to be energized when working tirelessly in service to others. There is a time and place for emergency heroics and forgetting yourself in the moment to reach out an assist another in need. Normally though, you owe it to yourself to formulate a conscious first imperative that makes sure you get what you need, if not in this moment, then very soon. You cannot love your neighbor without first loving yourself.

Winning and Losing

> *"This is not the end; this is not even the beginning of the end; this is just perhaps the end of the beginning."*
> — Winston S. Churchill

> *"Winning isn't everything—but wanting to win is."*
> — Vince Lombardi Jr.

Winning at all costs is another first imperative that governs a lot of lives. Have you ever gotten angry and even enraged when stuck in a traffic jam as you were rushing to be on time for an important appointment? Do you recall the anxiety you felt and the inability to think straight? What motivated this reaction? Often it is the need to win – or at least, to not be a loser. Winning is part of our need to control the outcome. If we can let go of our attachment to the outcome we become able to focus on the present moment with gratitude.

You may think you are settling for second-best when you say, "I didn't get what I wanted; I didn't win." But feeling like a loser is a perspective *you choose,* so why not choose a different and more positive one? Maybe you need a new first imperative to take care of the win/lose habit that says: "Life is not about winning and losing; it's about living and loving in order to find wholeness and holiness." This perspective enables you to always to view life in the "win" column no matter what the outcome. It neutralizes any notion of failure and the belief that your lives could be of anything but paramount value.

Beginning Again

Being true to a healthy and well-reasoned first imperative will invite many interruptions and disruptions. It requires us to begin again, and again and again. It may result in jettisoning long-held ideals and practices such as a religious tradition, a loveless marriage, or a career. Getting used to fresh starts in life can be another imperative, which, if we fully embrace it, will enable us to learn from our past and move into a brighter future.

My old first imperative had placed my emotional life on hold. It was born out of how I was treated as a young adult among peers. It held back my maturing process: "Protect myself from getting hurt no matter what." A new first imperative led me from dentistry to ministry: "The most important value in life is Jesus' teachings." Yet another has taken me out of parish ministry in order to serve as a life coach: "There are many ways I can help people transform their lives for the better."

Beginning again takes fortitude. It exhibits a massive amount of resiliency, a total surrender to the present moment. This requires dipping into the reserves of courage you may not realize you already have. Surrender is not giving up or throwing in the towel; in the spiritual context it means letting go of the past and of whatever is distracting you from your life purpose. Simply acknowledge that you have done the best you can until now – you have given it your best shot. Now you can let go and allow the Universe to communicate with your intuition to show you the next step to take. During this process, you may want to speak with a friend, counselor, life coach, or clergy person to get a fresh perspective. Then use your mind and heart to respond appropriately.

Surrendering in order to kick-start life is scary because it is *total,* with no strings attached, and unconditional. When you surrender you consciously choose to stop trying so hard to control. You become brutally honest, without shaming yourself, and admit not defeat, but the need to pause and to let go of self-justification.

Sometimes we surrender because we cannot go another step, and sometimes we surrender because we have tried every other possible way with no success. So when we get to that impasse, we do nothing but wait...and be present. Yet how do we surrender to the emptiness of not having or getting what we wanted or thought we needed? We need to remember that presence in this moment carries with it the consolation of forgiveness, integrity, self-compassion and hope.

FOR REFLECTION:

- How would you describe your first imperative?
- How has the perspective of winning and losing influenced your life?
- Are you being invited to begin again? What has to end in order to do so?

Chapter 4

Intimacy and Spirituality

"It is an absolute human certainty that no one can know his own beauty or perceive a sense of his own worth until it has been reflected back to him in the mirror of another loving, caring human being."

— John Joseph Powell,
The Secret of Staying in Love

A very important part of the process in learning to listen to our intuition and our inner truth is beginning to recognize the external *first imperatives* we have adopted in our lives. We often discover these imperatives while searching for a spiritual path that is the most meaningful to us.

Searching for a spiritual path so that we can become better versions of ourselves takes a lifetime. In our search for direction, many of us realize that our desire for God precedes all other desires; we recognize our need to be connected to a spiritual Source that is beyond all earthly life. Some believe we find this Source through organized religion. On the other hand, many do not hold to traditional religious ideas or even the existence of a God. Whatever our starting points, one thing we all have in common is our ability as humans to transcend ourselves, to reflect upon ourselves and upon the ineffable, and to move beyond our own consciousness to a greater collective consciousness. This transcendence is rooted in a quest for love-based spiritual intimacy.

We use the word "Spirit" because it is associated with the word for "breath." We breathe in the energy of the universe with every inhale. In letting go of the breath we let go of tension, of control, and of any concept of time. Concentrating on the breath means being conscious of the present moment as Spirit speaks to our hearts. When we breath consciously, we bring all of our relationships together into our heart as one, renewing force for our body and soul.

As children, many of us received conceptions about God and religion that we may have never questioned at the time and may have not since. Our parents, teachers, and clergy fed us a steady diet of imperatives that were meant to help us find God and stay in God's good graces. Often built into these imperatives and beliefs was the admonition never to question them. So we obeyed, following the path of least resistance and seeking the approval of religious leaders and parents as we followed the guidelines. During significant family religious events such as weddings, baptisms, or funerals we did as we were told by parents, spouses, and children, and we did not always stop to ask ourselves *what it all really meant to us personally*. We probably never questioned the imperatives.

Since I left parish ministry I have come to realize that what I intuit (the messages I receive through my intuition) and what I believe in my heart trumps *any* external imperative. I have come to realize that my priesthood is much broader and inclusive than that defined by the church. Many of the teachings of the church, when seen in the wider context of the universe, are pale reflections of the truth. Being defined as a Catholic is not as important to me as being in union with God by whatever means God wishes to offer. For me, traditional concepts of God and heaven fall far short of the reality of Universal Spirit and consciousness that we cannot come close to defining. Have I rejected religion? Let us say I have come to realize the severe limitations of all organized religions as well as their benefits to society. I simply choose to follow the lead of the Spirit.

I invite you now to question those imperatives that you still cling to and that are no longer serving your life. I want to get away from the magical notion that an external "good" Spirit, such as "God," somehow intervenes directly in the course of our life events or even worse, that an "evil" spirit, such as "the devil," has the power to influence our decisions and actions. In our hunger for spiritual guidance, particularly in a time of crisis or change, we ought to let our *personal experiences* and our journey *inward* determine our spiritual outlook; not the other way around. We no longer have to shoe-horn our lives with the preconceptions of any one organized religion or system. But in order to have a say in this, we need take the time to examine the background of religion, how it operates, and really look at how its first imperatives influence our lives. Then we are free to create our own imperatives that are truly in line with who we are.

In this chapter I will begin with how your family of origin can influence your ability to be intimate with yourself and others. I will then write about the many different ways in which you can express and experience intimacy. I will then delve into the matter of faith and intimacy with religion (so-called *revealed faith*) and the deeper experience of spiritual intimacy to which you and I are invited.

Intimacy and Family

> *"Hell, in my opinion, is never finding your true self and never living your own life or knowing who you are."*
>
> — John Bradshaw, *Healing the Shame that Binds You.*

True intimacy is an expression of our Spirit. Our desire for intimacy is an internal first imperative that we share as human beings. We can be led unknowingly, however, into fulfilling *external* first imperatives, that close us off from true intimacy. Often this occurs as a result of unhealthy family relationships.

We humans possess the fullest possible capacity for intimacy when we are newborns. At that point in life we have no filters that prevent us from connecting with others physically, emotionally, or spiritually. Then as we grow up, we gradually learn what it means to be wounded in Spirit and soul. In response to traumatic events we develop ways to filter out unpleasant encounters. This often means we start to close ourselves off and so, over time we become less open to true intimacy.

Many of us curtailed striving for intimacy due to dysfunction in our families. Sometimes the dysfunction manifested as a result of our adult care-takers having been previously abused and wounded. They couldn't do anything to prevent it at the time and we were unable to stop its ongoing toxic effects in our lives. To take back our capacity for intimacy we need first to understand *how* our family systems may have sabotaged it.

Family systems are always in a delicate balance. Psychologist John Bradshaw wrote in great detail on this subject in his landmark book *On the Family* (1988, Health Communications Inc., Deerfield Beach, FL). Dr. Bradshaw says that a dominant family member who has a major emotional or spiritual issue affects the entire family. The issue may be substance addiction, mental illness, abuse, domestic violence, criminal activity, or a disorder like post-traumatic stress.

Dr. Bradshaw explains that a person so afflicted in a family indirectly controls the mood and behavior of everyone else. As a consequence, all of the other members of the family automatically learn to unconsciously play their parts in order to keep the family in its diseased, but stable, balance. Even though everyone senses something is wrong, keeping the family together and functioning is of higher value than the happiness and mental health of the individual members.

In Dr. Bradshaw's analysis each person plays a role in keeping the family in balance. Someone, usually the spouse or parent, plays the enabler and aids and abets the problematic member. Another family member might take on the role of the "rebellious one" who gets the attention he or she needs by causing trouble. Another child might fall into the role of the "peace keeper," bending over backwards and forgoing his or her needs so as not to add to the family conflicts. And yet another family member might take on role of the responsible "hyper-achiever," appearing successful on the outside but secretly feeling crushed spiritually.

In Dr. Bradshaw's model, when everyone keeps to their roles there is a greater chance of peace, but it is at the cost of continued dysfunction. Yet as soon as even one member decides to get help and break out of the system, therefore upsetting the balance, there is hell to pay. For example, if someone in the family becomes sober or attends Al Anon meetings, or leaves home, or undergoes psychotherapy, the home dynamics are changed and the remaining members' roles no longer fit into the system. He explains that turmoil is often the result in this situation and, ironically, that the one who got help or who escaped the system is often the one who gets blamed for everyone else's problems. That person had dared to shine a bright light on the lack of true intimacy from which everyone was suffering.

Following the lead of Dr. Bradshaw's work, each of us, even in the most dysfunctional of relationships, need to *take care of ourselves first*. We may be seen as the "villain" who spoiled everything for everyone else or the lightning rod for future misfortunes in the family. Yet disrupting the *status quo* may be exactly the catalyst needed for everyone else to also get help. Either way, we have a primary responsibility to ourselves to get well whether or not we can bring others with us. I highly recommended Dr. Bradshaw's books because his insights into toxic shame and dysfunction were breakthroughs for me in understanding my own upbringing and the way it affected my relationships as an adult.

Authentic intimacy is Spirit's goal. It can only be found in heart-to-heart communication that has the potential to change you. It is no wonder that this quality of communication is called "social intercourse." It is a transfer of one-to-one heartfelt love from a place of being able to still maintain your individuality. Intimacy lifts you to a higher plane of human existence – to a more complete expression of love that goes beyond sentiment and physicality. It also moves you to serve the most vulnerable around you willingly and unselfishly because you begin to recognize your union as one with them.

Intimacy also places you in the midst of the universal energy that energizes you, helping you to realize how similar you are to a loving God. Through intimate relationship, you gain the vision and strength to promote the common good and you are able to develop skills in social intercourse. It is this social intercourse that cross-fertilizes ideas, hopes, dreams, positive change, equanimity, justice, freedom, and contentment.

Kinds of Intimacy

> *"Prayer is not asking. It is a longing of the soul. It is daily admission of one's weakness. It is better in prayer to have a heart without words than words without a heart."*
>
> — Mahatma Gandhi

We each have an instinctual longing for intimacy that never leaves us, even when it has been, or is being, violated or wounded. I recall vividly that as a child of about nine or ten I would wander into the woods near my home, particularly when I was feeling lonely. Going down the hill past the purple columbines, I would come upon a bubbling stream—"my stream"—banked by boulders, lush green ferns and Indian pipes. I would sit on the soft carpet of moss, take in the perfume of decaying leaves and moist earth and listen to the breeze rustling through the leaves. I felt protected in the intimacy of nature. Soon it was time to go home, but I always left with a bit of hope that, if I had felt embraced by the woods, perhaps I too had a place in the world.

Where can you get *your* dose of transcendent intimacy? It might not be the woods for you – it could be anywhere, at any time. We can find intimacy on many levels and in a variety of opportunities:

Physical intimacy runs the gamut from playing contact sports, to having a quiet meal with someone, to putting away the phone whenever in face-to-face conversation to acknowledging the presence of another being sitting next to us on the bus.

Intellectual intimacy happens when we connect in thoughts with ourselves or others. We experience it in our private thoughts, in our journaling, when we read a good book or whenever we share ideas, beliefs, and conversation with another.

Social intimacy promotes community values and personal friendships through common interests and mutual service. The act of voting, getting involved in justice issues, serving on a jury, or just being kind to the cashier at Walmart creates the kind of intimacy that builds and strengthens mutual respect in community.

Emotional intimacy offers a glimpse into the eternal as well as into our inner lives. Those with whom we share our feelings likewise invite us in to know theirs and how our presence adds value to their lives.

Spiritual intimacy centers our hearts on our deepest-held values, beliefs and perspectives that bring us out of ourselves into a more profound and universal love and peace.

Sexual intimacy brings together all of the above modes of intimacy. It is ultimately *physical*, bringing out the best of our wild, passionate nature. It deepens connection on all levels and commitment between partners and has the potential at times to create new life. It is profoundly *intellectual* because great sexual intercourse flows naturally from great verbal intercourse. It is *social* because it can be a starting point to new, yet unexplored aspects of a relationship, bonding couples with their extended families and relationships. It is also movingly *emotional* because the very act of making love, entered into with sensitivity and openness, offers both partners a fuller expression of their male and female energies and the full range of human feelings. Sexual intimacy is also supremely *spiritual*. Some of the saints, such as St. Teresa of Avila and St. Julian of Norwich, have candidly described their transcendent experience of God's love as orgasmic. The energy of erotic love, which is at the heart of our creativity and generativity, enables a primal transcendent connection with another's Spirit. In that moment of connection we sense what Michelangelo depicted in his *Creation of Adam* on the Sistine Chapel ceiling: the experience of Eros—of life-giving Spirit—that is our uniquely human Soul.

It takes courage to be intimate. When we open yourself up time and again to intimacy, despite how many times we have been hurt, and no matter the deep wounds we may carry are, we allow communication free reign and learn that vulnerability is the key to happiness.

On the other hand, if we deliberately sabotage intimacy, we actually invite conflict. The Jewish Holocaust of World War II Germany began with the Nazis driving a wedge between Jewish Germans, who had been part of the fabric of daily society for centuries, and the rest of the German population, most of whom were Lutheran or Catholic Christians. Nazi propaganda, persecution and labeling undermined the very humanity of the Jews and also of homosexuals, the mentally handicapped, Jehovah Witnesses and any religious and political leaders who dared question the regime. They were all sent off to concentration camps where they were enslaved, starved, and gassed to death. The German citizenry accepted the fate of their confreres because the Jews had been objectified as objects of scorn and as economic oppressors. The Nazis effectively dismantled the social, spiritual and intellectual intimacy they had previous enjoyed with their neighbors. This is almost always the first step in the process of a small group of individuals gaining control of the power structures of the majority. We still see this in 21st century societies. We witness it every time a bully pushes around his or her weight.

I want to remind you, as I do my coaching clients, that the most important gift God has given you is...you. You may tend think that only God, your partner, children, parents or even career hold this place in your life. Yet *you* alone are the only gift that keeps on giving to yourself! And, you can *take back* your power from religious authorities, parents, and teachers who may have abused your individuality, freedom, and individual conscience by promoting conformity at your expense.

Spiritual maturity based in true intimacy helps you realize that it is not your responsibility to work for or achieve some level of trust in God. Instead, you can simply accept yourself as you are and, if our trust allows, you can open yourself to the transcendent Spirit that consistently loves you.

This trust must begin with yourself and with valuing your uniqueness and personal dignity above all else. As difficult as it is, you have to embrace every aspect of your life – even the unattractive parts and even the times when you miss the mark (sin). You must do so without conditions, judgment, or the nagging suspicion that there is something wrong with you. Instead, develop the nagging conviction that there is *everything right about you!* If you want to live a life of contentment and fulfillment, this has to be your baseline position for existence – your primary imperative.

Ultimately, if God is complete and eternal, then God is not really interested in our prayers or in our striving toward some kind of perfection or in our self-loathing. Instead the Universe seeks only our growing capacities to love, to be grateful even for the negatives in life, and to forgive ourselves and others. As we build these capacities, this we bring about a transformation in the world.

I also do not believe for a moment that God can ever be "offended" by our stupidity, mistakes in judgment, or even deliberate stepping out of line. God simply places these matters back in our laps for us to resolve in a just and honest way. If God, as defined by many religions, is supreme, then

God also knows that we will miss the mark, just as a parent expects an infant to spill food from time to time. And for those inclined to believe in an afterlife, a threat of "losing salvation" or "not being forgiven" could never be present in the mind of a loving God.

Revealed Faith

> *"I believe in Christianity as I believe that the sun has risen: not only because I see it, but because by it I see everything else."*
>
> — C.S. Lewis

> *"My religion is very simple. My religion is kindness."*
> — Dalai Lama XIV

One spiritual connection many of us seek is intimacy with God – with the transcendent. Religion alone cannot create this intimacy. It hopefully facilitates it and offers help along the way toward it but religion cannot replace a heart-to-heart encounter with Spirit.

Most religions normally rely on what is called "revealed faith." This is a list of beliefs that is thought to come directly from the mouth of God. In most religions, the list was codified by an overarching religious authority such as a group of prophets, preachers, imams, rabbis, or bishops. These official authorities wielded a great deal of influence since they determined membership in the religion by what was to be believed.

The idea of a faith that has been revealed from on high enables religions to maintain, at least outwardly, a cohesive and consistent message. The message is meant to support the community of faith so that members exercise genuine love and visible care for each other. But the opposite is also true: The failure of formal religious communities to offer genuine support and love to members in need can be a stumbling block to their spiritual growth.

For a majority of Christians, part of revealed faith is the concept of *sacrament*. Celebrating these rituals is supposed to bring spiritual help or grace to the individual, strengthening their faith and commitment to God and to the community. Sacraments such as baptism and holy communion consist of tangible and physical signs such as water, bread, and wine. These signs are revered by the community as coming from God and imbued with deep spiritual meaning.

Yet often a magical view of sacrament and ritual prevails. There is usually an emphasis on what God is doing for the believer through sacred actions, but not the other way around. Often ignored is the need for the believer to have *already been transformed* by the transcendent for the ritual to have any coherent meaning.

One major downside of revealed faith is that it is usually open to multiple and often confusing understandings that force members to pick and choose which to believe. Embedded in these interpretations is usually the expectation that they must live up to the religion's moral and spiritual ideals or blame, judgment and punishment are inevitable. Traditional religious morality, especially in the West, is built on a dualistic view of life as being good or bad; holy or sinful. This dualism does not take into account the grey areas where apparently wrong behaviors, especially in the realm of sexuality, may actually lead to good and holy results.

Some kind of sacred text is usually at the heart of revealed faith. This text is supposedly from God and recorded through human agents. These texts are used for information and inspiration and form the basis of most religions.

Some religions accept sacred scriptures at face value – word for word, as if they need no interpretation. Others use historical context, form, and current theological understanding to tease out the deeper spiritual meaning behind the words. The job of interpreting scripture usually falls to a local or regional leader whose teaching is meant to keep members of the religion on the right track. Their status as leaders gives them a leg up on everyone else as they exercise teaching with authority and governance. Yet despite all of these carefully crafted layers in religion, none of them, even taken together, creates an intimate relationship with God.

When revealed faith becomes an end in itself it enters the realm of "fundamentalism." This is a general term to describe absolute adherence to a set of doctrines on faith and morality, as well as adherence to a fixed interpretation of scriptures, that together become a litmus test for true believers aiming to be destined for a happy afterlife. In a community based on fundamentalist doctrines, the saved are separated from the unsaved.

Religious fundamentalism appeals to people who look for unambiguous and absolute answers to faith questions. They tend to fit objective reality into their narrow religious world-view. This world-view tends to foster conflict between religion and science as well as hostility with the modern world, medical practice, psychology, other religious opinions, personal conscience, and equality of the sexes.

As you will see below, there is a spirituality that simultaneously promotes your relationship with the universal presence of God *and* enables you to connect with your inner guidance for direction so you can freely express the truths in your soul. Let's dig deeper.

Transcendence and Intimacy

> *"Most people are slow to champion love because they fear the transformation it brings into their lives. And make no mistake about it: Love does take over and transform the schemes and operations of our egos in a very mighty way."*
>
> — Aberjhani, *Journey through the Power of the Rainbow: Quotations from a Life Made Out of Poetry.*

If we have ever sensed a spiritual hunger, it is because we yearn for intimacy with the transcendent. Fundamentalism often replaces this intimacy with a ready-made, sometimes slavish adherence to an external religious system. It tries to put God into a neat, easily reproducible package supported by scripture proof texts, tradition and dogma, and ultimately, limits personal freedom. Unlike the facile definitions of God enjoyed by many fundamentalists, we may have to admit that no one can really define what God is all about, given our limited human capacity. Ultimately, we have to examine *our own hearts and minds* to discover that spark of transcendence – that prompting to move beyond ourselves in order to touch the infinite.

Religion only acts as a safe container for us to put our collective spiritual experiences that define our personal faith into. It has become a measuring stick against which we determine our personal value. But there is nowhere to get to; we are all on a journey – we are not already at the destination seeing a neon sign flashing over the pearly gates. This seemingly "safe container" of religion is actually empty; without spirituality, religion is a lifeless corpse.

The intimacy Jesus spoke of is the deepest hunger of the human Spirit. It is both an energy that fills us and a driving force that propels us. It moves us to form connections that bring about mutual transformation. The quality and depth of our experience of intimacy defines who we are and whether or not we acknowledge that we have a purpose in life. Faith flows from intimacy and a trust that intimate connection will result in positive change.

In reframing our concepts of God and religion, it is important we keep our focus both on the practical *and* the mystical – on action *and* contemplation. True faith always seeks change and moves us closer to personal integrity and to service. Richard Rohr, a leading Franciscan spiritual author, says it well:

> *When religion does not move people to the mystical or non-dual level of consciousness it is more a part of the problem than any solution whatsoever. It solidifies angers, creates enemies, and is almost always exclusionary of the most recent definition of 'sinner.' At this level, it is largely incapable of its supreme task of healing, reconciling, forgiving, and peacemaking.*

*When religion does not give people an inner life or a
real prayer life, it is missing its primary vocation.*

— Richard Rohr, *Breathing Under Water*, p. xxiv

The inner life of the Spirit ultimately leads us to knowing ourselves better and moves us to a mystical union with all others around us. Our starting point may be awe and wonder of the natural world, a profoundly moving relationship with a person, living or deceased, or even the growing self-awareness of your own unique beauty.

Intimacy and transcendence are the two goals of spirituality and the ultimate purposes of our lives here on earth. This leads me to offer a personal reflection on intimacy and transcendence from the *Gospel of John*, chapter 17. Use this discussion to delve more deeply into your own experience of transcendent intimacy.

In his gospel, St. John the Evangelist describes Jesus as the source of mystical and transcendent intimacy. He cites Jesus' "high priestly prayer," uttered just before his death on the cross. In some ways it can be viewed as Jesus' last will and testament. Here Jesus spoke of the intimate, cosmic nature of his consciousness as united with God's consciousness and with that of his disciples' (quotes are from the *New American Standard Bible*):

> Lifting up His eyes to heaven, [Jesus] said, 'Father, the hour has come; glorify Your Son, that the Son may glorify You, even as You gave him authority over all flesh, that to all whom You have given him, he may give eternal life. This is eternal life, that they may know You, the only true God, and Jesus Christ whom You have sent. I glorified You on the

> *earth, having accomplished the work which You have given me to do. Now, Father, glorify me together with Yourself, with the glory which I had with You before the world was.'*

Jesus' three-year public ministry was all about being a conduit for God and transforming the minds and hearts of the people he touched. His relationship with God was like that of an only son and his father, who sent Jesus into the world as an expression of glorification. Glorification was more than a perfecting. It was a *transformation* that enabled Jesus to transcend time and space.

Jesus then prayed:

> *'I ask on their behalf; I do not ask on behalf of the world, but of those whom You have given me; for they are Yours; and all things that are mine are Yours, and Yours are mine; and I have been glorified in them. I am no longer in the world; and yet they themselves are in the world, and I come to You. Holy Father, keep them in Your name, the name which You have given me, that they may be one even as we are.'*

Here, Jesus took glorification a step further. He considered his disciples extensions of himself and of the Father. To him, they were conduits of his intimate and transformative love. They would complete his ministry in God's name, "Yahweh," or, *I Am Who Am.* To him, God is always fully in the present moment and so likewise should be his disciples.

He continues:

> *'But now I come to You; and these things I speak in the world so that they may have my joy made full in themselves. I have given them Your word; and*

> *the world has hated them, because they are not of the world, even as I am not of the world. I do not ask You to take them out of the world, but to keep them from the evil one. They are not of the world, even as I am not of the world. Sanctify them in the truth; Your word is truth. As You sent me into the world, I also have sent them into the world. For their sakes I sanctify myself, that they themselves also may be sanctified in truth.'*

Revealed faith continues to think that the sinful world is at odds with the perfection of heaven. Jesus rejected this notion. He did not want to remove his disciples from the world. Instead he wanted to perfect the world through their intentions and actions. The disciples would be purified by their faith in Jesus, the Word of God in the flesh. He sent them into the world ("apostle" means *to be sent*) on a mission. That mission was to bring together the rest of the world in an intimate knowledge of God.

Jesus also emphasized radical oneness through the eternal transforming power (glory) of love:

> *'The glory which You have given me I have given to them, that they may be one, just as we are one; I in them and You in me, that they may be perfected in unity, so that the world may know that You sent me, and loved them, even as You have loved me. Father, I desire that they also, whom You have given me, be with me where I am, so that they may see my glory which You have given me, for You loved me before the foundation of the world.'*

Jesus' message was about unity, transformation, and love. His intention was to place ultimate responsibility on each of us to serve the ends for which he prayed. Jesus also spoke of his disciples as a community; he sent them out together as a sign of their mutual love and support.

As you reframe your concepts of God and religion what seem to be the new priorities on which you will spend more time and effort? Moving toward integration and authentic spiritual encounter is your goal. What will make that goal viable for you, even if it creates a bit of controversy among the ones you love?

FOR REFLECTION:

- How has your view of God changed over the years?
- Describe some ways in which you enjoy intimacy.
- How does Jesus' prayer in John's gospel reframe your concept of God and religion?
- How has intimate love made a difference in your life?

Chapter 5

Making Friends with Loneliness and Fear

"Solitude is fine, but you need someone to tell that solitude is fine."

— Honoré de Balzac

"When I get lonely these days, I think: So BE lonely, Liz. Learn your way around loneliness. Make a map of it. Sit with it, for once in your life. Welcome to the human experience. But never again use another person's body or emotions as a scratching post for your own unfulfilled yearnings."

— Elizabeth Gilbert, *Eat, Pray, Love*

When my mother died in 1999 after a two-year battle with lymphoma I experienced and still experience to this day, an emptiness I had never known. Suddenly the one person who was unreservedly prejudiced toward my welfare was gone. I also felt relief that she was no longer suffering, and felt liberated that I no longer needed to worry about her and that she did not need to worry about me. But there was still a tremendous amount of grief that I experienced from the loss. The grief then turned into loneliness.

My loneliness and grief led me to get away for a vacation in Palm Springs in the winter of 2000. At the age of forty-eight, my trip was primarily to resolve some of the loneliness I was experiencing and also to find out more about myself as a gay man. I stayed in a gay-owned resort motel for a week and from there I explored the rugged terrain, the restaurants, and the male scenery. After a week of living differently than I ever had, and experiencing what I had never felt, I sensed my loneliness lifting as if the beginning of my life had arrived.

Many of us think of loneliness and fear as negatives – experiences that are to be avoided at all costs. But while momentarily unpleasant and stressful, they can be carriers of important messages. If we listen with our hearts in those times, we will discover that loneliness and fear are actually friends who show us where we need to grow.

In this chapter I will make the distinction between being lonely and alone and how you may be called to the latter as an important means to deepening intimacy. I will then speak of the legacy that fear leaves behind, the power of anxiety and grief, and overcoming fear and anxiety. I will end with steps you can take toward courageous and life-changing action in your life.

Alone or Lonely?

I love reruns of the "Twilight Zone." I find some of the best episodes perfectly depict the effect on individuals of being totally alone and abandoned on a distant planet or after a catastrophic event. The episodes show that being alone is ripe with meaning as we are confronted with our individuality and our longing for connection and intimacy in those moments.

For centuries, spiritual men and women have chosen to live solitary lives, living alone and apart from daily social interaction. By doing this they felt freed from distractions so they could commune with the transcendent. These "hermits" and "desert dwellers" discovered the secret in loneliness. When being alone became too intense they would use the feeling to explore their depths of intimacy. They learned to make friends with loneliness and gave it a voice of its own. This voice cut through the layers of justification, rationalization, and fear common to humanity and led them to discover the place in the heart where both the light of perfect joy and the darkness of pride reside.

You are likely not a hermit, a monk or a nun living in a desert cave or monasteries. This means that in your busy world, if you want solitude you need *actively to seek it.* This may mean deliberately moving away from your tablet, phone, earbuds, and television from time to time in order to slow down your mind enough to let in the messages carried by loneliness or fear.

At first being alone may feel scary, but soon the quiet and the lack of sensory stimulation will open up pathways to the heart. When loneliness sets in it can feel like fear. Human beings naturally fear isolation and abandonment – we fear being forgotten, devalued, or discounted. Yet neither loneliness nor fear are terminal; they cannot harm us. We can invite loneliness into a relationship with us as if it were a person living within us. We can express our reactions to the loneliness and ask it what it is trying to tell us.

Loneliness asks us to examine our fear. We do not come by most of our fears by accident; they often live in our bodies as a result of some trauma, large or small. They can become like habits, such as what happens in the case of phobias. Fear also can be based in falsehoods, misinformation and bigotry. Such is the case when segments of society fear racial, religious, or ethnic groups. Fear is also taught: Children easily pick up on their parents' fears and can live them out and pass them down to the next generations.

Most of us do not want to confront fear head-on. We sometimes wait for someone to rescue us so we do not have to. Our culture states that neither men nor women are supposed to be fearful; it is often portrayed as a sign of weakness. Yet waiting to be rescued can get people into all sorts of codependent trouble. There are some who prey on the fears of others as a means to control and manipulate them. Thus as painful as it may be, it is always best to admit our fears out loud and begin to address them, if necessary with a coach or therapist. We need to acknowledge them and discover their origin. A primal fear, especially in today's overwrought and information-saturated society, is the fear of being *different*. When we do not feel as if we fit into the norm that is being propagandized in our culture, we end up thinking something is wrong with us. As a result, we feel isolated and devalued and like we are traversing a tight rope without a net – one fall and we are finished.

The fear of being different and therefore not being accepted produces a surfeit of loneliness and grief. Escaping these feelings is a motivation for substance abuse, depression, or even suicide. It is even more serious for gay, lesbian, and transgender youth, who are trying, often alone, to understand why they do not fit into the "norm" or why they simply are not being accepted for who they know they are. Their suicide rate is several times the national average for their age group.

Loneliness and fear are like the canary in a mine, which dies when the oxygen is getting low, warning miners to ascend to the surface in a hurry. Loneliness tells you that your Spirit is suffocating. It appears whenever you are overworked, overwhelmed with responsibilities, or imbalanced in your giving to others and not taking care of yourself. When loneliness shows up it is not to make you feel sad; rather, it is a signal that something important in your life needs your attention and that you deserve better.

When you address loneliness as a friend you take away its power to play on your fears. Imagine loneliness as the voice of your soul, speaking to your mind through your heart. Ask loneliness what it has to say about your inherent value, about your vulnerability and about your sense of wonder and awe for your universe. Listen to loneliness tell you that that you are going to be alright. In doing so, your fear dissipates and you no longer feel quite so abandoned.

The Legacy of Fear

"We must learn to regard people less in the light of what they do or omit to do, and more in the light of what they suffer."

— Dietrich Bonhoeffer,
Letters and Papers from Prison

Fear has a life of its own, often showing up as clinical phobias. Fear stresses the body's nervous system and puts us in a semi-permanent fight or flight mode. We often manage to trick ourselves into short-circuiting the stress with activities that flood our systems with brain chemicals that calm us and offer a sense of well-being. These are the hormones that have the narcotic effect that we get when we exercise or hike through the forest – they also get released when we turn to food, sex, alcohol, drugs, internet surfing, shopping, video games, and anything that occupies the portion of our minds that "changes the emotional channel" temporarily.

Fear prevents us from living authentically. When we give in to fear, we no longer live in the present moment and instead focus on what might be coming next, thus producing a constant stream of stress hormones such as adrenaline and cortisol, in our bodies. Our minds continually worry about what we want, need, expect, desire, demand, or can tolerate. And coming from this place, when we do not get what we expect in any given situation our inner Spirits can devolve into a sea of anger, resentment, hurt, bitterness, sadness, and depression. This is akin to narcissism – the conviction that the entire world owes us something.

The most unfortunate result of this constant presence of fear is that the present moment comes and goes with little notice. Living in the future, planning the next step, taking a defensive posture, and trying to outwit fate is a poor substitute for living in the here and now. When we are fearful we ignore the opportunity for joy. We live in the illusion that we are ready for anything, all the while fearing that we may still have missed something in our preparedness, and that something terrible might happen to us.

You can rescue yourself from fear by focusing on the present moment with gratitude and examining the messages your mind is telling you. "Re-mind" yourself that you are wonderfully creative and whole and that it is not worth wasting your energy on continuous mental analyses. Start to replace pipe-dreams of what *should be* with appreciation for what you have and *who you are*. You can cease searching for that perfect relationship that will complete or give ultimate meaning to your life, and learn simply to be your fullest and true self, without apology, in or out of a relationship.

Anxiety and Grief

What is it about anxiety that makes it so common? Anxiety disorders are almost at epidemic proportions and they are defined in as many ways as are the individuals suffering from them. Dr. David D. Burns is a cognitive therapist who wrote *The Feeling Good Handbook* (Penguin Books, 1989). In it he writes that there are three competing theories about the causes of anxiety. He writes that: "A *cognitive therapist* would claim that negative thoughts and irrational attitudes cause anxiety. *Psychoanalysts* would argue that repressed conflicts make you anxious. Some *psychiatrists* think that it is an imbalance in your body chemistry that causes feelings of fear and panic." (page 209) In other words, we feel anxious when our thoughts race through possible disastrous scenarios, when we feel victimized by a situation or sometimes when our blood sugar drops and we need simply to eat. Anxiety can also be a free-floating gut feeling that something is wrong and we cannot put our finger on it.

Sufferers of anxiety often feel isolated and lonely, as if no one can understand what they are going through. They may experience a tightness in their shoulder muscles or abdomen, headaches, or beads of perspiration forming on the brow – although they do not know exactly why. Anxiety is debilitating because it can keep sufferers awake with obsessive thoughts, paralyzing them from taking action. It can deepen the fear of the unknown in a kind of "fear of fear." Anxiety sufferers worry about how they might react in an imaginary situation, experiencing many of the symptoms of stress before anything actually occurs.

Recognizing the root causes of anxiety can be difficult. We have been given the message that we ought to be competent, in control and have our act together at all times. We thus tend to push anxiety aside as a temporary problem rather than seeing it as a bearer of information. But anxiety, just like loneliness and fear, carries important messages with it. Anxiety, if we listen to our hearts, will reveal the unspoken messages that swirl around in our bodies and minds in anticipation of an event, or as a result of an incident over which we had no control. We need to put words onto those experiences, process them, learn from them and get them out of our heads.

Grief is similar to anxiety in that it grabs us by the throat and does not let go. When changes occur in life—when we lose something of value or when we are forced into a transition we did not expect or ask for—grief inevitably follows. Grief and loss are manifestations of loneliness and fear and carry anxiety with them. Grief shows up as a by-product of relationships that are not going well or that have ended. We may experience grief as a result of losing someone we love through death, dementia, alcoholism, or mental illness. We may feel profound fear when we hear that someone close to us is not going to recover from an accident or illness. Any kind of change in a relationship, in the way we view ourselves or in the expected outcomes on which we counted tears a gaping hole in the fabric of our emotional lives that takes time to reweave. Grief is part of the process of discovery and healing after events like these.

Grief has effects on our bodies: For one thing, it impairs our senses, making us unsure of ourselves and causing us to be unable to fully function. It also has a way of making us feel as if we will never come to the end of it – that we are destined to experience the pain of grief and loss for the rest of our lives. It is this that sends many people into depression and despair.

Our first duty to ourselves is to let grief and loss *unfold* – to accept that we cannot avoid it in the moment that we are experiencing it. We need to be with others as we grieve. In many cultures, professional grievers have been hired throughout history to wail and weep at the funerals of loved ones. They were surrogates who did not just act but who bonded emotionally with the family's experience in that moment. They were needed and supported the process. The same is true of wakes and funeral rites that to many seem superfluous but can be of great emotional solace to the ones grieving the loss.

For grief to be effective, you need to give your entire selves over to it – physically, emotionally, verbally, and spiritually. Bluntly express how you feel to yourself and to God/ the Universe. Pull no punches. You must clear your emotional landscape and rebalance your internal chemistry in preparation for the greater message that grief has to reveal to you – one that is far greater than that of abandonment: the message of *hope* and *change*.

Overcoming Fear and Anxiety

In sudden situations, fear propels you in one of two directions: It can push you to take dramatic remedial action as you put your life on the line for others, such as saving a person in a burning building, or it can paralyze you. How can you act courageously in a mindful, conscious way when you are experiencing fear? Doing so takes practice and addressing each of your fears separately. This exercise may be helpful for you if you struggle with anxiety – yet note that it does not replace professional intervention if you need it.

Five Steps to Courageous Action

Start by breathing slowly and deliberately and focusing on your breath. Inhale through your nose and exhale through your mouth throughout this exercise.

First, identify and acknowledge the actual feelings you are sensing. Name them and then allow them to have space in your life and your body for the moment. Look for the origins of one of the feelings in your body. What does this feeling remind you of? What other uncomfortable incident produced this fear or anxiety? Acknowledging the familiarity of the feeling gives you the space needed to take the next step. Keep breathing.

Second, ask for help. You can get support for this from a good friend who understands you or from a professional such as a coach or therapist. Express the source of your fears to this person in order to have them acknowledged as normal by someone you respect. Focus on your feelings, giving free range to your emotions so that you can express tears, anger, or loud expressions and can release them from your body. Ask your friend to check in with you as you move through the next steps toward courageous action. You may have to go back for additional emotional releases along the way, as strong fears may need more than one resolution. Breathe.

Third, call up the uncomfortable feeling once again and calmly name the situation or incident for what it is, resisting the temptation to make it sound like the worst possible event ever, or as if it "always happens to me." Instead, calmly describe in words how the incident makes you feel in the present moment. Breathe.

Fourth, determine what the next good move ought to be. Break it up into small, manageable steps. For example, what do you need to do to protect your legal rights, finances, a valued relationship or a fulfilling job? What core values of yours do you want to be aware of and preserve in the situation? What does your intuition tell you about the next appropriate move or action? Breathe.

Fifth, put into action the decision you made. Do not look back and second-guess yourself. Take the plunge forward into the unknown, even if you think your decision will produce predictable results. Also be open to the surprise, the unexpected and the proverbial "wrench in the works." If something happens to throw you off, or you are still feeling paralyzed by fear, go back to the first step and work through this process once again, as dispassionately as possible and with as much patience as you can muster. Breathe some more!

Being courageous has nothing to do with forcing yourself to be heroic or taking huge risks. Courage is simply *self-reflecting and taking appropriate action in the moment.* It is not extraordinary – in fact, people show courage every day when they say and do the right thing at work, home, and in their relationships. Courage is about stepping out of your routine emotional reactions—putting them aside for a moment—and thinking through the situation as dispassionately as possible. Then, when you take the action that you determine is best, and follow through with it, you transcend your fear.

FOR REFLECTION:

- If loneliness were a person, how would you speak to it?
- What do you think loneliness and fear would tell you about yourself?
- What do loneliness and grief tell you about taking care of yourself?
- What are some messages you can give yourself each day to remind you of your ultimate worth and value?

Chapter 6

Our Deepest Desires

"Thou hast made us for thyself, O Lord, and our heart is restless until it finds its rest in thee."

— Augustine of Hippo, *Confessions*

"All men want, not something to do with, but something to do, or rather something to be."

— Henry David Thoreau, *Walden*

We do not really know ourselves until we know the deepest desires we hold in our hearts. Only in knowing our deepest desires can we enter into the spiritual intimacy we seek.

Expressing these desires may seem at first to be inappropriate. After all there are so many people with needs in the world and so many going without the necessities of life. You may be wondering, "What right do I have to desire anything more than the basics I need in order to live each day?" But, although it is true that many do not have their needs met, this does not negate that we still need to express our desires. Otherwise, what we harbor in our hearts goes undercover. The desires we do not express turn into subconscious, free-floating hungers and veer us off track when we least expect it. Our desires attempt to get lived out in some way, clouding our life-focus and distracting us. Repressing them can also hurt others and even land us in jail if we live out our fantasies through inappropriate or unethical actions that threaten our closest relationships, interfere with our work, or block true intimacy. I like to say that desires of the heart eventually "squeeze out the sides" like jelly out of a sandwich if they have nowhere else to go.

Our job is to make them explicit; to put words to our feelings, as crazy as they may sound, and to bring even our darkest desires out into the light. We should use professional help to do so if necessary. When we do this, we can tease out the meaning in them, understand the deeper issues they symbolize, and potentially even see deeper desires they may be masking.

Expressing the desires of our hearts, even if we think we cannot attain them at the time, enables us to examine the underlying motivation behind them and identify their relationship with our life's purpose and with our goals and dreams.

In this chapter I will discuss with you how to make your deepest desires more explicit. I will also look with you at the limiting beliefs that keep you from your true calling and talk about the role integrity plays in the expression of what you really want.

Discovery

How do we discover what our true desires really are? When I was a senior in college I began thinking seriously about a career shift to ministry. How did I know that it was something God wanted for me? At the time, a respected friend from *Seekers* told me to imagine having absolutely no obstacles in life, no money problems, no pressure from others and no limits. Then he said, "Now, ask yourself: *What is my deepest desire for my life?*" A few months later I took myself out of the application process for dental school and applied to the seminary.

There are a lot of distractions that can keep us from identifying the desires of our hearts. Mind chatter is one of them. It is the *polar opposite* of the language spoken by our hearts. Most of us are familiar with mind chatter: words, phrases and internal debates, all shouting at once in our heads. Mind chatter usually happens when we have nothing important or immediate to think about or when we are overloaded and stressed and want to escape through distraction. If you have ever done some extended task alone such as mowing the lawn, folding clothes, or driving on familiar highways then you know how mind chatter can fill the void.

Our hearts are the epicenter of your Spirit and emotions. It is from there that we receive non-verbal messages that we can hear through the power of our intuition. We can sense that they are authentic because they feel right and true to us. We cannot just jump in feet first, though – we have to test our messages by giving ourselves time to ruminate on them and by checking in with trusted coaches or counselors. We need to sit with them and allow them to take up the space they need in order for us to be able to articulate them and accept them fully.

Two essential elements we need as we listen to our heart's messages are brutal honesty and curiosity. We have to be *willing* to hear the difficult message – possibly the very message that makes us look squarely and uncomfortably at we you have been living up until now. We have to want nothing less than complete truth about ourselves. We must believe that articulating our deepest desires will flesh out our purpose for living. We must ask hard questions and imagine the possible scenarios and the options of we you might act with courage. We must always seek the truth.

Your heart will speak to you with familiar words and concepts *if you give them space to do so*. First you have to go silent – to a place where there are no distractions, where you can be alone with your thoughts and where you can put the mind chatter to rest. This becomes more and more difficult if you fill every moment of every day with sounds and sights that stimulate the mind and suffocate the heart. Plan for your quiet times and find somewhere you can go to be alone like an empty church, a quiet museum, a favorite trail, or a rock by the lake or ocean. Doing so sets the stage for your Spirit to speak from your heart.

Once you have spent a few moments in quiet, ask what you need to ask and wait for an answer. Our hearts are so used to being relegated as second to our minds that it might take some time for your heart to find its voice. When it does, it will tell you what is going on and will indicate that a deep desire has been rummaging around in your life without an outlet.

You can use prayer or meditation for this process known as "waiting on God." This can be a wonderful practice because the deepest desires of your heart are authentic indicators of what the Universe desires for us. They tend to bubble up in meditation, as long as we do not drown them out with verbiage. God knows what is in our hearts without our needing to tell God. Your desires have been there since you came into existence waiting for your heart to have the opportunity to make them explicit.

Our life experience enables us to put words to and flesh on our desires. Some desires prove to be transitory or end up being dead ends. Others burn hot and then cool down into hobbies. One or two might key into the source of our life purpose. They say something about who we are, what priorities we seek, what values we are willing to live and die for and what dreams we want fulfilled. Our souls are more attuned than our minds to what we really need.

Sometimes we first have to address the needs that are more obvious to us, such as hunger, shelter, friendship, safety, intellectual satisfaction, creativity, or even a new car. Only after "clearing the decks" from distractions will we be ready to identify our deeper needs hidden in the language of Spirit, love, and transcendence. At that point we are ready to place the palm of your hand on your heart, take several slow, deep breaths, and ask ourselves: *In this moment, what will give ultimate meaning and purpose to my life? What is the true desire of my heart?*

In this process, you may encounter some inner voices that tell you that you cannot have what you want, that your life is not that important, that you are not enough or that you are too much. These saboteurs also come in the form of fear, anxiety, and stress and limit your ability to dream the big dreams that embody the starting points for the next phase of your life. They, too, need to be addressed and put in their place, using the sage voice of your heart's wisdom to counteract their effect.

Reflection on your deepest desires will evolve, especially in light of circumstances such as illness, the loss of a loved one, a divorce, or a major shift in career. Yet even in the midst of turmoil and especially *because* of turmoil, you can still decide on the life you really want. You can determine the degree to which you are comfortable with the commitments you have and may choose to limit or broaden them depending on how they fit into your deepest desires. In both cases, courage and decisive action are necessary for you to exercise lest you leave room for others to decide for you what your desires ought to be.

What if you have already been following your heart and have made some irrevocable decisions about marriage, children, locale, finances, or career choices? Ask yourself, which of these are non-negotiables that are permanent parts of your life? Which can you imagine setting aside or changing in order to be in alignment with the current desires of your heart? With whom can you share your reflections to receive honest and loving feedback?

Limiting Beliefs

> "The world is little, people are little, human life is little. There is only one big thing — desire."
>
> — Willa Cather, *The Song of the Lark*

I once met an attractive woman who was interested in finding a life coach for her daughter. It seemed that the young lady had made a lot of unfortunate life decisions and at the tender age of 24 was involved with an abusive partner. Mom thought that her daughter's poor judgment stemmed from her father dying when she was very young. It seemed as if the young lady had allowed the limiting belief that her father had abandoned her to determine the kind of man and relationship she thought she deserved.

A belief, whether conscious or unconscious, becomes "limiting" when it is used as an excuse or justification for the decisions we make or the stories we tell about our lives. Empowering limiting beliefs renders us victims of circumstances that we actually made up in the first place. Limiting beliefs become emotional crutches that we rely on and internalize as part of who we are.

Many young men of earlier generations, such as myself, developed the limiting belief that they were no good at playing sports. This was due to male stereotypes regarding strength and prowess, the insensitivity of school gym instructors who did not assist those of us who were less coordinated, the focus on team sports at the expense of solitary activities for boys and an attitude of condescension toward academic types. Many of us were simply shamed and made to feel like constant disappointments, even embarrassments, to our jock instructors, fathers, and the popular guys in school. Some of us even defaulted to a hate of sports as a defense strategy in response to feeling "abnormal." We internalized the criticism and the defense strategy.

Limiting beliefs have a direct pipeline to our hearts and nervous systems. They train our bodies and Spirits to respond to false assumptions and to externalize them. They are negative intentions that get fulfilled because they have a choke-hold on our core beliefs about ourselves.

What we call "beliefs" or "truths"—even those based in religion—may actually be just fabrications we or others have imposed on us. Some of these activate fear, guilt, and a feeling of being defective whenever a thought, person, or event triggers us. The beliefs live in our bodies as physical energy and affect our emotions and moods. We give the beliefs great power when we depend on them to justify our decisions that keep us safe, show our worthiness or get us a reward. But none of the beliefs are real, and they all undermine our Spirit.

If you feel unhappy about your life, that might be why. You may be relying on limiting beliefs and stories to protect you from harm and may be heaping expectations on others to make you happy. Many a destructive dysfunctional relationship began with limiting beliefs and both partners seeking completion in each other.

You know that person you know who is always complaining? Try asking them, "What do you believe about yourself that seems to be making you so unhappy?" This may be the one question they have never asked themselves. But be prepared for the floodgates to open, as they may share with you many years of pent up limiting beliefs that they have since made into dogmas that they have allowed to control their lives.

If you can make up a sad story or put a negative spin on an event so that it has a life of its own, then you can do the same with a good story and a positive spin. Beliefs that do *not* limit you and that build up your dignity, talent, beauty and inner strength can change your internal storyline and allow you to be content with who you are. You can choose new beliefs. It is in your power.

Five Steps to Smashing Limiting Beliefs

What can you do to identify and transform your limiting beliefs so that you can dream more deeply about your deepest desires and so effect the disruptive shift you may need?

First, identify and choose one limiting belief at a time. I suggest choosing the one you feel defines your life, the one that you do not want to let go of, or the one that holds you back the most and creates the most pain for you.

Second, look for one or two other possible meanings for this belief. For example, if you hate sports, think of a reason other than your performance that you might hate them – maybe because of the fear of disappointing someone or letting yourself down.

Third, choose an *uplifting*, *empowering* belief to replace the painful, limiting one. Sometimes choosing the *exact opposite* of your limiting belief will work, but not always. It has to be something realistic that you *can* believe even if right now you do not believe it one hundred percent. For example, *I enjoy playing in the local softball team* may not work. *I look forward to taking a brisk daily walk for fifteen minutes* may do the trick.

Fourth, each time this old belief shows up, tell yourself that you no longer choose this belief and that you are only willing to look for evidence that would show that the *contrary* to this limiting belief is true.

Fifth, look for this contrary evidence many times each day and remind yourself to practice this several times each day. It only takes a few minutes a day to do this.

This process requires that you be present with yourself. You need to slow down enough to pay attention to what you are actually saying to yourself as a background story in your life and to see the events and people that help to reinforce it and keep it alive. You may discover that your limiting beliefs—not just your emotional wounds—are responsible for your not moving forward the way you want in your relationships and your career. The ultimate goal is to create limitless beliefs that allow you to fully be the creative and whole persons you truly are.

Integrity

Personal integrity is both paramount and the ultimate goal when it comes to making sound decisions based on our deepest desires. When we act based on our limiting beliefs, we are out of integrity with our true selves. On the other hand, when we let go of limiting beliefs, our integrity with ourselves is intact. I always thought I was a person of integrity until I examined the many ways in which I wriggled out of taking responsibility and blamed others for my disappointments in life. I had a stack of limiting beliefs that reduced my choices. I used to use my own brand of logic, my background in history and my knowledge of theology and spirituality to justify myself. I lacked integrity. In some ways I was a fraud.

Integrity is a primal first imperative. It calls us to fulfill our basic need to be whole and complete. We develop our integrity "muscles" by going inward and aligning our thoughts, feelings, and actions with our true selves and desires. We go through cycles in our lives of being connected to ourselves and then falling away from our desires and vision. During these cycles we need to trust the process and take with us the only currency we have in this world: our *personal integrity.*

Although integrity is personal, it is not something you can hold on to as your own or achieve by sheer will. It is a quality only others can see and recognize in you; you can only hope that you are showing it through your words and actions. If pride gets in the way, your integrity and authenticity immediately come into question. In challenging moments, ask yourself: *In this moment, am I bringing forth consciously the totality of who I am without prejudgment, ready for the next right thing?*

In this adventure we need pure hearts, open to our own brokenness and unmet expectations, free of self-sabotaging pride, and receptive to the unexpected gifts of the Universe.

FOR REFLECTION:

- What have you discovered are the deepest desires of your heart?
- What limiting beliefs have kept you from pursing your deepest desires?
- What actions will build up your personal integrity?

Chapter 7

Choosing This Moment

"The past has no power over the present moment."
— Eckhart Tolle, *The Power of Now*

"Life will give you whatever experience is most help-ful for the evolution of your consciousness. How do you know this is the experience you need? Because this is the experience you are having at the moment."

— Eckhart Tolle, *A New Earth: Awakening to Your Life's Purpose*

The only moment we have is this one. Living in the present is not as common as it used to be when people aligned their lives with the movement of the sun, the change of the seasons, and the inherent helplessness encountered in disease and relatively shorter life-spans. Today, we need to *practice* living in the present because our fast-paced world, artificial environments, and the fact that we are all on communication overload tend to push us constantly into the future.

How we treat the present moment has a spiritual ripple effect throughout time and space. We experience this phenomenon as we witness the effects of human activity on environment and on countless species of plants and animals. Through our actions we are even training deadly bacteria to become resistant to medications.

In this chapter we will examine the power of living in the present moment. I will ask you if you are open to making changes in your life and new decisions that might contradict your previous life choices. Finally, I will discuss the beauty of vulnerability and end with Michael Beckwith's *Four Stages of Unfolding*.

The Power of Now

One of the most life-changing books I have ever read is Eckhart Tolle's *The Power of Now* (Namaste Publishing, 1999). Tolle is a Swiss-born Canadian who explains his transcendent existential philosophy by showing us how to focus totally on the present. He challenges people of faith to believe that if there is a higher power, all good will come to pass. He says that each of the interconnected nanoseconds of this present moment has meaning. As soon as one passes, there is only the next nanosecond, nothing more; the future has yet to reveal itself. This is also the message of the Buddha, Christ, and others spiritual mentors.

Living in this moment as a first imperative is the key to finding self-love. When we see ourselves suspended in the perfect time and place of this moment, we cannot help but cherish our unique being-ness, our precious existence and our all-embracing self-awareness of being a vital and unique part of the universe.

Seeking the "now" moment is the first step to discovering the deepest desires of your heart. When your meditations uncover a gut feeling that something is emerging it ought to prompt you to stop and gather your consciousness in that moment. When you do this, you put yourself in a position to ask help from the Universe and quiet down any distress you may feel about the situation you are in. You can breathe and just listen.

These moments can lead to profound discovery that leads to change. The key is to seek the meaning of the now moment for its own sake without preconceptions about how it may change your life. The trick is to simply quiet down and focus, laser-like, on what your heart is telling you, without judgment or fear. Open your consciousness to the sights, smells, sounds, touches and tastes you are experiencing. Quiet the voices in your head, put aside your stress and let the next moment take care of itself.

Daily Decisions

A married couple from my first parish was involved in preparing couples for marriage in the church. They once told me something I have never forgotten: "Love is not a feeling or emotion; it is a daily decision." What they meant by that is that love is always experienced *in the now* and that the marriage relationship lives in a daily, conscious intention.

Choosing to live in this moment, whether as a single or partnered individual, means being very clear about how you we choose to relate to the world.

As an individual, you need to come to a decision as to your life purpose and what unique gift you offer that adds value to people's lives. This requires a degree of self-reflection that a lot of people shy away from. It requires mental and spiritual work for which you will need to make space in your life. Otherwise you will, like so many in our fast-paced world, simply react to daily encounters and circumstances.

The spontaneity of reacting might seem attractive at times but it can drive you from event to event without a chance to breathe. The whole purpose of this book is to help you interrupt the flow of events in your life and to disrupt your instinct toward too spontaneous of a reaction that inherently robs you of your true self-expression. The challenge—and gift—in the present moment is for you to stop and determine the best action that will move you to the next moment; not to simply default to a thoughtless reaction in response to the last moment.

Shifting to the Next Moment

The present moment ultimately gives way to the next. We can choose to flow into the next moment without reflection, or we can embark on a journey of discovery about how the present moment has made us more aware of our having changed.

You are not the same person you were a nanosecond ago. Whatever you experienced in the past that led you to be currently reading this book is the raw material of transformation that is making a positive difference for you now, and subsequently will make a difference for your future.

Something from the past is always the catalyst for change, but the intentions we previously had are no longer applicable. When we truly live in the present moment, we see that we may not be able to maintain old commitments, and if we do, we will be approaching them in a new way. The present moment will always call us to move on to the next moment whether we are ready or not, so we had better be ready. We can prepare by adopting an attitude of awe, wonder, and curiosity and by putting aside any sense of dread or foreboding. This makes the next moment more of an adventure and less of a fearful "unknown."

We sense the call to the future with some trepidation, nostalgia, and maybe relief. We have to face up to the collateral damage from past decisions that may have effected innocent parties. I recently spoke with a friend whose parents had divorced when he was a small child. He had not been in contact with his father for the last sixty years. His father remarried and formed a new family and made no attempt until recently to contact him. He was surprised to find out that he had four half-siblings. His elderly father sent a plane ticket for him to visit. When they met, they exchanged handshakes and his father spent the rest of the visit alone in his room. He could not move on to the next moment. He was stuck in his past. Though holding no resentment toward his father, my friend inevitably returned home feeling empty and incomplete.

At times, you are going to make a mess of your life and it will affect others. It is unavoidable. These are the times you must forgive yourself and those around you. You may go through difficult times of loss or grief or may have to uncover truths you have been keeping secret such as your sexual orientation, an addiction, an emotional health issue, or a call to explore life anew. In these moments, you must not only embrace the present, but look to and embrace the *next* moments that you can not only look forward to, but deserve. They are your second chances at life and happiness, despite any regret you might feel about collateral damage.

Crisis

> "The strongest love is the love that can demonstrate its fragility."
>
> — Paulo Coelho, *Eleven Minutes*

When change calls, crisis follows. Crisis comes from the Greek word meaning decision, choice, election, or judgment. Each personal conflict we have can be an opportunity to decide to love, to choose to communicate more deeply, to elect to be open to new feelings, and to acknowledge ourselves and others as worthy of our time and effort. It is in crisis that we learn to be vulnerable to how we truly feel. In crisis we get to share our feelings honestly and candidly. We can lay out our realities and what we are experiencing in the now, no matter how painful it is to do so and without prejudging how anyone else will react in response.

It is a human trait to avoid crisis. To try to avoid it, we fill our lives with concrete goals and achievements that will reward us emotionally or financially. These benefits may give us immediate gratification but they may also blind us to our need to make a decision about something – a choice that will determine the next phase of our lives.

Just as I experienced in the priesthood, many of us feel trapped in a stale job, overwhelmed with responsibilities and sick of routines that we could do in our sleep. We may have internalized our stress and may be injuring our health. In our culture, we learn to be passive-aggressive to avoid confrontation and get our way. For example, if we are unhappy at work, we may simply quit without wanting to ruffle any feathers, run away from our current workplace and try to find a new job.

The same may be true in personal relationships. Marriages can grow stale, friendships end and relationships shift. In our current culture, heartfelt and honest communication seem like quaint Victorian concepts. Boredom and indifference act as smoke screens that anchor us in the past and neutralize our dreams. Relationships that avoid crises at any cost are dying. We are meant for new challenges and meant to grow and interact with others without shame.

You may have to finally admit that even when you have consistently laid everything out for examination and discussion in a relationship, the commitment to love on either your side or the other may have run its course. Admitting this also strikes at the heart of vulnerability. In these situations, it is like you have reached a pause—a semi-colon in the flow of life—and it does not feel good, but it is real, vulnerable and should be embraced.

The now moment is asking you to reflect upon interruptions like these, discuss them and not assume you must take action quite yet. Sensing that you have come to the end of the line in a marriage, friendship, or business partnership may be an opportunity for you and the other person to restart the relationship on a different, more authentic level. These pauses are opportunities to look within your soul and to honestly assess who you are meant to still walk with on your journey and who your confidants may be. You may discover that the person to whom you were once married is now a much better friend. And yes, your kids eventually will understand if you and your spouse help them to process their feelings about the split by looking at the positives that will come out of the evolved relationship.

Vulnerability and Spontaneity

> "Owning our story can be hard but not nearly as difficult as spending our lives running from it. Embracing our vulnerabilities is risky but not nearly as dangerous as giving up on love and belonging and joy—the experiences that make us the most vulnerable. Only when we are brave enough to explore the darkness will we discover the infinite power of our light."

> — Brené Brown

None of us enjoys being vulnerable; it feels like being naked with all eyes staring on our least attractive physical features. Most of us, particularly men in our society, do anything it takes to hide our vulnerability or deflect attention off of it altogether. Yet our deepest, most profound changes happen when we allow ourselves to be "seen" and when we reframe our perceived weaknesses as strengths.

Vulnerability and spontaneity go hand in hand. In the present moment we cannot afford to hesitate when a blessing or gift presents itself to us. We need to practice saying "yes" as a first response. When we open ourselves up to the full range of possibilities in any given situation, we discover paths we have not yet traveled that can ultimately change us and our lives for the better.

We also need to exercise *prudent reflection* on when best to be vulnerable and spontaneous. Prudent reflection is another way of listening to our intuition to determine if the new course feels right according to our core values. We need to ask, *What might be the best course of action right now?* We need to listen for the action that will best serve us in our vulnerability. Being vulnerable is a way to act upon our daily decision to love ourselves.

The urge to be spontaneous in the midst of serious vulnerability caused me to ask myself in 2009, *What do I really want for my life?* In that now moment I heard my heart say, *It is time to go.* Despite my concern that I would receive no pension if I left the priesthood, I knew in my heart that I needed a new life. I had to leave the system of a church that I had once loved but that now was eating away at me from within.

You may feel you struggle with being "appropriately" vulnerable and spontaneous. What gets in the way of taking the right action is the tendency to default to older habits that feel comfortable, familiar and safe. Embracing your vulnerability gives you strength and let's your Soul speak.

The Unfolding

As life spreads out before us, no decision or choice need be permanent. There is no need for our minds to be at war with our hearts. As we unfold into the space and time granted to us in this moment, we can let go of the extremes of rationality and emotionalism. Michael Bernard Beckwith, pastor of Agape Church in Los Angeles, speaks about how our lives unfold like a video on *YouTube*. He reminds us that it is not all about what we can get out of life, but, rather, about inviting the Universe, God, or Love, to be increasingly revealed through the unfolding of our unique and individual souls. He says that life is about celebrating being one with each other and God.

He also tells us that we are here to reveal our magnificence and that we get to participate in our unfolding if we so choose. Beckwith describes this process in his *Four Stages of Unfolding:*

Stage One: The Victim. If we are honest with ourselves, we know that we have gone through periods in our lives where we have felt like a victim. We may even embody the victim now; our being may be identified with victimhood. Being the victim means that we are allowing something outside of us to determine our happiness or destiny. As victims, we manufacture victim stories to blame someone who has "made" us unhappy. In this stage we tend to experience not reality as it truly is, but in accordance with our thinking about reality. We ruminate over past offenses and we weave them into the fabric of our individual biographies. We end up feeling short-changed in life.

Stage Two: The Manifestor. In this stage Beckwith tells us that we begin to be responsible for our lives, our thinking, our perceptions, and whatever flows out of our mouths. As a manifestor, we develop an intention for the kind of lives we want to live and the sort of relationships and qualities we wish to enjoy. As we create intentions they begin to unfold in our lives. In this stage, we allow the vibrations of our deepest desires to be congruent with those most desired for us by the Universe. At this point we get out of our own way and start to make things happen.

Stage Three: The Channel/The Instrument. Here we become the means for spiritual insight for others, deliberately welcoming it and not just allowing it to happen. In this stage, we begin to reflect and to reveal the infinite and the transcendent. We yield to it and surrender to it. We stop fighting what God wants for us and instead make peace with our lives. As channels, we are not victims; life is on our side.

Stage Four: The State of Being. Our sense of being separate from God, from life, and from love dissolves in this stage. Beckwith describes that in this stage our lives become one with the infinite. We begin to embrace the reality that there is only one life in the universe and that we, and everyone else, are all individual expressions of that one life. We welcome forgiveness because all forgiveness is self-forgiveness. We realize that hanging on to resentments and hate manifests more of the same because our internal vibrations bring them into reality.

During our unfolding, God calls us to surrender and to give up control – something most of us hold precious. Yet, it can be a *gentle* surrender – a gradual, incremental giving over.

Through this process, you are called to give up your blame/victim stories and your personal sense of separation from life, from God, and from joy. You have the power within you to replace your toxic mind stories with heart stories that offer you hope and life, and most of all enable you to focus on the now.

FOR REFLECTION:

- What is the most difficult part of being in the "now" for me?
- How have relationships changed in my life and evolved into something different?
- Do I sense more satisfaction based on who I am or on what I do?
- At what stage of unfolding am I?

Chapter 8

Change: The Only Absolute

You must be the change you wish to see in the world.
—Gandhi

When we live in the present moment the one thing we are guaranteed is change as we move into the next moment. Our lives are in constant flux and the major disruptions we experience are often merely the cumulative result of the imperceptible changes that have been happening from moment to moment.

As we invite change in our lives, we also invite a continuous clarifying of our values by which we govern our lives.

As you move through change, you may suddenly realize that some of the values you held dear for years are no longer worth the effort and sacrifice it once took to maintain them. But what you may think are inconvenient interruptions in the flow of your life that upset the *status quo* are actually just the result of your life revealing itself more fully. While this is happening, you may get a shiver of awe and wonder, *Why me? What is going on?* But it is just the natural flow of your life unfolding in the present moment.

The only absolute is change. In this chapter I will look at how the voice of change speaks to our ultimate good. I will discuss the role and importance of personal conscience in shifting your approach to life. We will also see what happens when the values we embrace clash and when we have decided we have had enough. I will end this section with talking about the call for alternative life-plans and leave you with a famous Jewish parable.

Conscience

When our hearts tell us how to behave and on what to base our personal values, we call this our *conscience*. Our consciences continually goad us into accepting change. If we allow them free rein they will speak to us of new ways to love and serve through the expression of our core values. Our consciences may say things to us like: *Either get involved or move on. Make a choice and act on it with your deepest conviction.*

Especially when we encounter crises, we begin to discover others who think and act as we do. We have the tendency to join spiritual forces with them in proclaiming our core values and want to unite with them to form a community. This phenomenon is at the heart of every political revolution and large-scale change that affects a whole nation. We do the same on the small scale in our lives, usually when something dramatic has happened and we can no longer rely on the traditional allies of religion, family, social status, or career. We seek new allies in the midst of crises – men and women who will support us as we live out the prompting of our consciences.

Major change always brings about a flurry of ideas as to how best to proceed. This is the time to get good advice. The people you discover along the way who understand where you have been and who have been there themselves are the ones you need on your side. Some of them may even surprise you as you may have even once viewed them as adversaries. Who are the psychotherapists, life coaches, clergy, family members, kindred spirits and friends on whom you can count?

Even with allies at your side, your conscience will be sensitive to hearing opinions or approaches that differ from yours. You may even feel threatened by someone else's point of view about life, God, religion, or love, however logical, articulate, or well-formed it may be. In these moments you are being invited to slow down, to take time to listen and not respond, lest you are tempted to strike back or dismiss others as ignorant or narrow-minded, missing what their hearts are trying to communicate to you. By listening, you may learn something new; you may even alter your own beliefs. Despite our firmly held absolutes about something, there is in fact no one "right" answer after all.

What happens to many of us in the midst of change is we expand our spirituality to become more inclusive of a wider range of convictions toward relationships, the body, sexuality, and transcendence. As we move through change, we discover more and more that our consciences are happiest in the in-between, grey areas of life. Absolutes and "black and white" thinking become irrelevant to the way life actually unfolds. We may even find, as I have, that we stop trying to define God in mere words and instead open our hearts and mind to an infinite spectrum of spiritual experiences.

When Enough is Enough

A few months before he died in 2009, my father said to me, "If you ever have to leave the priesthood, it's okay. Do what's best for you." I appreciated his realistic candor and support. He always gave me the freedom to do what I thought best. Within a year I did decide to leave. Yet many of us were taught never to give up – to see through a commitment to the bitter end; otherwise it did not demonstrate a well-formed character. Because of this widely-held belief, we endured the criticism that we were not trying hard enough knowing all along that something was seriously wrong. I am reminded of a scene in the film *Gallipoli* where the British command continually sent Australian troops over the hill only for them to be shot dead by enemy machine gun fire as soon as they reached the crest. Hundreds of infantrymen died for nothing because their commanders neither waited patiently for the right moment or circumstances to attack nor chose a tactical retreat. They simply continued with the same plan, no matter how destructive it became.

The inner call for change eventually becomes deafening if we wait long enough. When it arrives, we can either ignore it, blame others for our crisis or recognize the emotional and spiritual pain we are in and do something to take care of ourselves. I left parish ministry behind to begin a new life when I realized that in forty years I had changed and the church had not. I needed also to admit that I originally chose this vocation in part because my personal history prompted me to seek a neat, unambiguous box in which to place myself. I wanted a simple, clear, and regulated focus for my life. Over time I had to admit that the church's "one size fits all" policies governing priests' assignments did not work for me. The box was suffocating me spiritually; *enough was enough.*

Coming to the admission that enough is enough takes a great deal of courage. We do not like to reach this point and hope instead that the circumstances surrounding our personal or professional lives will improve sufficiently for us to maintain life as it is.

Yet if *you* are the most important gift God has given you, you *owe* it to yourself to declare an end to fighting a losing battle. There is nothing wrong with retreating or with surrendering to forces that you cannot control and that you know will ultimately harm your Spirit.

I Am Enough

"Enough is enough" is a valid strategic position to take in life. You are worth so much more than any one relationship you have, any particular calling or any one job or career. Reaching your limit somewhere and knowing that a new direction is necessary is a *gift.*

Having to change direction in life requires that you recognize another truth: *You are enough.* You are complete, whole, sufficient and infinitely valuable just as you are in this moment. This sounds like a trivial truism until you absorb these words in your heart: *I am enough.* Saying these words to myself still makes me shed a tear or two of awe and wonder. I am often amazed by my own fierce resiliency.

This message is the *opposite* of what we hear in the world. The message out there is that *we are not enough until* we earn that next degree, until we pay for that next certification, until we train for that next skill set, until we develop a professional network, a business plan and a six-figure salary, until we pay off our debts, until we become the ideal spouse or parent, until we have the ideal body, or until we purchase that new home or car. We work to please others and to fulfill their expectations, and we pray to God that they—whoever "they" are—will eventually notice and pay attention to us.

The sense of not being enough and the need to please others in order to feel accepted is deeply embedded in Western culture. Our modern-day norms for middle- and upper-class family life emerged out of the nineteenth-century Victorian era. The Anglo-Saxon style of raising children was idealized and prevailed in most of the English and German-speaking worlds, including North America and South Asia. In this paradigm there was a sharp divide between the adult world and the child's. Mothers and children were viewed as extensions of the patriarchs, the male heads of the households. They were like ornaments or possessions meant to bring honor to the family.

For children to be recognized as full persons they had to pass through fixed steps along the way to adulthood. Male children were often considered not enough unless they proved themselves by working up the ranks in their father's business or joining a branch of the military and fighting in a war. Female children were not enough until they married as virgins into the "right family," produced a houseful of heirs and sacrificed everything for their husbands whom they vowed to obey absolutely.

This rigid paradigm began to soften with the tragedy of World War 1, the recognition of a woman's right to vote in

1920 and child-labor laws. But the residual effects of these cultural habits have lasted through to today. They can be especially seen in the lack of equal pay for women doing the same jobs as men and the continued preponderance of child labor and human trafficking. Today many would call this Victorian paradigm emotionally and morally abusive.

More recently, many children receive the message that they are not enough unless they live up to certain stereotypes of male or female behavior or body image. Some feel "less than" because they are growing up in poverty, or even homeless, are part of a racial, ethnic, or religious minority, are living without parents, are struggling with poor nutrition, suffer from undiagnosed emotional or behavioral issues, or depending on government assistance. Stereotyping has been institutionalized in some communities and is still being ignored or discounted by government and school officials.

Children may also sense that they are *less than* if serious family dysfunction, addiction, abuse or bullying dominates their homes. All of these things and more can prevent tender souls from developing a properly aligned emotional self-awareness. Instead the abuse and shame causes them to feel defective as persons. As adults they may expect someone or something to complete them and define their worth. Many end up in the court and penal systems. It all comes from the feeling of *not being enough*.

Related to feeling that we are not enough is the sense that we are *too much*; that our uniqueness does not fit in and that there is something wrong with us.

When you feel this way, your psychological profile, your sensitivity, your emotional energy, your inquiring mind, your bold opinions, your masculine/feminine balance, your way of communicating, your talents, your interests, your friends and your habits...they are just too much to take! Being too much is at the heart of our culture's struggle to accept diversity in sexual identity, sexual orientation, racial identification, religious practice, and any other characteristic that does not blend easily into mainstream Caucasian Christian America.

As a child, you may have gotten the "you are too much" message from adults who did not understand you or your temperament. You may have been a "wild child," totally unselfconscious and adventuresome, or extremely introverted with an old soul and an intellect beyond your age. You may be homosexual, or may have felt growing up like you were a girl in a boy's body or a boy in a girl's body. You may have also felt out of sync with the world and culture around you and even ashamed for not quite fitting in. You may have carried those perceptions into adulthood.

In whichever way you may be emotionally wired, when you believe your life is sufficient the way it is, you have a greater chance of moving forward without looking back. *You are not too much for yourself; you are already complete and whole–* and that is the only person who really matters. Others will simply have to get used to you, provided we are not purposely antisocial or destructive. You can set intentions for yourself with the well-founded hope that the right result will come along in its time. You can come to believe in your heart that *you really are enough.*

How might you shift your perspective and invite the change that will allow you to feel that you are just enough as you are?

Five Steps to Being and Feeling Enough

First, get in touch with your infinite value and worth in the universe. Tell yourself: *The greatest gift God has given to me is my life.* Let go of hyper vigilance and looking over your shoulder for someone to correct or disapprove of you. Adopt the attitude that you are whole and complete, saying the words out loud, until it truly sinks in. Stop comparing yourself to others. "I am perfect the way I am." Repeat this out loud five times a day.

Second, verbalize a positive and clear intention for how you want your future to look. Ask yourself what the deepest desire of your heart might be. Picture yourself succeeding in what you want to do as a career. Imagine yourself with the kind of healthy relationship you truly *want* – not what you expect based on your past experiences.

Third, live in the perspective of *taking* rather than *asking*. This sounds counter-intuitive or even selfish, but in reality it is good self-care. It is easier and more powerful to take what you want with positive action and clear communication than to ask for it and wait forever for it to be bestowed on you from on high.

Fourth, be direct and clear about what you want. Do not self-sabotage by being too subtle or careful as to how to ask for something or deep down not believe that you will get it.

Fifth, *say what you mean and mean what you say.* After sufficient reflection and clarification as to what you really want, express it with *conviction* so that it comes from your core rather than simply being an interesting thought.

Fix This

> *"I must try to see the difference between my picture*
> *of a person and his behavior, as it is narcissistically*
> *distorted, and the person's reality as it exists regard-*
> *less of my interests, needs and fears."*

— Erich Fromm, *The Art of Loving*

I grew up hearing about my parents' difficult childhoods – they both lost their mothers at an early age, had to go to work at the age of fourteen and lived in relative poverty. In response, I felt as if I had to make their lives better and so strove to be a "good little boy." I tried to make them happy. I tried to fix them. And I hoped that if I earned enough "points" someone would fix me too.

Believing we need to be fixed or that we need to fix others contributes to our feeling of not being enough. It can also distract us from knowing when we have had enough. We are naturally happier when we can let life unfold, be detached from the words and actions of others and surrender to the outcome.

The need to fix and be fixed and the belief that we are not good enough, or that we are too much, can become internalized. These beliefs are like bullies living inside us. Some life coaches call these and many other such inner bullies and voices saboteurs because they interfere with our moving forward. They conspire to take us down. Saboteurs can heighten your sense of entitlement to the point of narcissism, causing us to use our gifts or authority with questionable motives. They compel us to justify our existence and actions on a daily basis.

Instead of focusing on what you have to do to become worthy, why not assume you are *already worthy?* Take the perspective that you are ready for consistent change and for unexpected blessings, without needing to control the outcome. You need to be present enough to be aware of spontaneous moments of surrender whenever they appear. Your expectations will always be exceeded as you open your mind and heart to the fulfillment we can derive from a single experience.

Many of us create our own little worlds of hopes and dreams. We become wedded to outcomes formed in our minds rather than possibilities that emerge from our hearts. By doing this, we end up cheapening and discounting the actual world around us. As a result, we may try to fit career or vocation or relationship into who we think we ought to be, *rather than seeking a good match for who we actually are.* Are you holding onto expectations and outcomes that you think you will "grow into" or that will "grow on you," instead of letting them go and finding your true path in life?

Cognitive Solutions to Depression

Striving to be enough can be a major saboteur when we are feeling overwhelmed. This struggle can lead particularly to situational depression which may be made worse by the conflicting messages we are getting and giving ourselves about being enough, or being too much.

If you are waking up in the morning with a feeling of dread, of feeling like you have to slog through another day, you may be in need of a good therapist or coach who will help you identify the real source of these moods. When you do not recognize when you have had enough, and that you *are* enough, you need to either change your perspective, or it is likely that you will continue feeling unhappy.

I have found *cognitive therapy* to be very effective for situational depression. Dr. David D. Burns' work, *The Feeling Good Handbook* (Penguin Books, Ltd., 1989) has been particularly helpful. Inspired by Dr. Burns, I offer my own list of destructive patterns of thought that caused my own situational depression. Being aware of them is the first step in taking away their power to influence our thoughts and moods. Here is my list:

Wishing upon a star. Melancholy thrives on magical thinking. In magical thinking, we think that if we believe hard enough and trust in some benevolent force, that our dreams for life will hopefully come true. When they do not, our disappointment leads to feeling unvalued, ignored, or left out.

Poor me, the Victim. An unattractive but prevalent and tenacious habit, feeling like a victim lays the foundation for cognitive dissonance. When in the victim mentality, we are automatically pitted against the world in which there are sinister intentions and conspiracy theories, and in which there is indifference toward our needs and lots of shaming.

Idealistic expectations. This is "Wouldn't it be nice if..." thinking at its worst. It is compounded when we also insert an idealized universe based in a religious interpretation. These expectations will back-fire nearly every time.

Pipe dreams and romantic reverie. Daydreaming is a great escape but can also emphasize the disparity between life as it is and as it should be in our "perfect" world. Ultimately it means that our lives are not enough.

Lack of emotional boundaries. This plagues everyone, especially those who are highly sensitive. Do you fail to establish the filters that regulate external stimuli? Without emotional boundaries our sense of empathy goes wild; we sense deeply the emotions of others around us and we can become overwhelmed, leading us to depression.

Comparison and envy. These habits tap into righteous indignation and trap us in a continuous analysis loop. The loop looks something like: *I'm not like her; she's more successful; I wish I was more successful; I wish I was more like her; but I'm not like her.*

I am not enough, or I'm not good enough. In this state of mind, no matter how hard we try, no matter what we are given to work with and no matter what good things others say about us, we do not believe we have what it takes to please others, to meet their needs, to find a relationship, or to get validation and recognition for our accomplishments.

Cause and effect spirituality. This view undergirds a lot of religions. It is a warped understanding of grace that came from the misinterpretation of scripture and from ignorant but well-meaning parents and preachers. In this view, we do not really believe in the free gift of God's love. Instead God will not help us until, and only if, we live up to God's ideal expectations of us and "please him."

Plan B

Relieving depressive thoughts can make room in our lives for hopeful ones. One way we can increase our "hope quotient" is to dream big dreams and to have a plan on which

149

we can fall back in case our first plan does not work out. By having a "Plan B," we admit that there are few "once and for all" decisions.

As a life coach, I help clients move from where they are in the present to where they want to be. I use powerful questions and other tools to help them identify and overcome obstacles that they have unwittingly erected in their paths. In order to counteract the saboteur that says, "You have made your choice, now stick with it and suffer the consequences," I recommend that my clients formulate a Plan B.

Plan B first and foremost assumes that *change is possible.* The decisions you previously made with your whole heart and pure intentions may not stand the test of time and experience. You may need to interrupt the flow and switch courses in your career, vocation and relationships.

Your career may now be flowing along in this moment better than you thought it would. According to the U.S. Bureau of Labor Statistics, 2012, the average period people hold a job is four to five years. That means that during a period of forty years we might change jobs between eight and ten times. The concept of a "job for life" with which we Boomers were familiar is gone. Not only is it natural for you to have more than one, or even several, job changes, those job changes, as well as shifts in your personal life, can in turn take a toll on your relationships – even the most stable of them. You need a Plan B.

A majority of gay men and women I have met in the Boomer age group suspected they were gay or lesbian but fell in love and formed a traditional marriage anyway. They had children and grandchildren and left the marriage only after a long period of confusion, indecision, and fear. They could no longer live as if they did not have a predominantly same-sex attraction, even though in most cases they truly loved the man or woman they had married and had been wonderful and nurturing parents. They needed a Plan B.

We all come to a deeper understanding of who we are over time. We also develop the faculties we need in order to address these issues maturely and fairly. We need contingency plans for our lives that take into account major career, relationship and financial shifting. We need to provide for being taken care of in sickness or old age. Plan B solutions offer a layer of support for the big changes we might have to make in our lives and sometimes beginning all over again.

I am relieved I had a Plan B because of the following unforeseen issues during my thirty-two years as a priest:

- A brain operation to remove a benign tumor that left me totally deaf in one ear and with irritating tinnitus in my head
- The church's handling of clergy sexual abuse of minors
- Not being provided an outlet for my talents and skills in ministry
- My experience of indifference toward me as a unique individual
- A lack of visionary leadership in the church institution

Your contingency Plan B will vary from others' depending upon your commitments, circumstances and your ability to dream. It may include basics such as writing your will, naming a person in your life with power of attorney, forming your living will and naming a health care proxy, and buying life insurance to cover dependents or your home mortgage in case of sudden death. It may mean looking for a safe house in the event you are being seriously threatened. Your Plan B may also be in the realm of a mental construct that may never be acted upon. The knowledge that it is waiting "in the wings" can relieve stressful moments.

A Parable

I will end this chapter with a story from Chassidic literature (*Tales of Hasidim* Vol. 2 by Martin Buber, ed. by Bonnie Fetterman) that illustrates the importance of knowing that there is no one, "right" answer when responding to change.

> The Master teaches the student that God created everything in the world to be appreciated, since everything is here to teach us a lesson. One clever student asks, "What lesson can we learn from atheists? Why did God create them?"
>
> The Master responds, "God created atheists to teach us the most important lesson of them all – the lesson of true compassion. You see, when an atheist performs an act of charity, visits someone who is sick, helps someone in need and cares for the world, he is not doing so because of some religious teaching. He does not believe that God commanded him to perform this act. In fact, he does not believe in God at all, so his acts are based on an inner sense of morality. And look at the kindness he can bestow upon others simply because he feels it to be right.
>
> "This means," the Master continued, "that when someone reaches out to you for help, you should

never say, 'I pray that God will help you.' Instead for the moment, you should become an atheist, imagine that there is no God who can help, and say 'I will help you.'"

All you have in this moment is yourself, your talents, your skills, your good will, your integrity, your faith, and, most of all, your ability to change and accept change as the only absolute. When you acknowledge this truth, you are ready to truly serve your highest self and your fellow man. You discover transformation and all else falls away as unimportant.

FOR REFLECTION:

- What changes have you found most challenging, but were most rewarding?
- Are your dreams based on who you are or who you want to become?
- How are you trying to fix your company, business or family without first accepting yourself as whole and entire?
- Have you formulated a *Plan B*? What circumstances can you imagine taking place that would require you to implement it?

Chapter 9

Healthy Boundaries

"When we fail to set boundaries and hold people accountable, we feel used and mistreated. This is why we sometimes attack who they are, which is far more hurtful than addressing a behavior or a choice."

— Brené Brown, *The Gifts of Imperfection: Let Go of Who You Think You're Supposed to Be and Embrace Who You Are*

We adults often approach life like it is a set of children's nesting blocks that we think ought to fit together in one pattern only. In contrast, many toddlers will find dozens of ways to play with such blocks and be very pleased with themselves in the process. It is we adults who abhor chaos and who will come along and nest them compactly and in perfect form before putting them away. Some small children have their own way of doing things and allow their growing and glowing intelligence to move them beyond the confines of any boundaries imposed on them. When as parents we try to define their personal boundaries, they tell us that they really do not "belong" to us and that they are unique individuals. This is an example of boundary setting.

In this chapter I will discuss the concept of personal boundaries – living within them and stretching beyond them. This section will help you to clarify your boundaries as based on your values. Then I will walk you through how to building healthy boundaries in your life. I will also address artificial boundaries that we have imposed upon ourselves: the bully within and needless suffering. I will end this section with examining a global, compassionate view of life.

Clarifying Boundaries

The concept of "personal boundaries" was new to me when I first read about it in codependency recovery literature. In reading about it, I discovered that for some of us our personal emotional boundaries too easily let in the energy that comes from other people's feelings and reactions.

You get a taste of this if you find yourself reacting strongly to fictional characters in novels or films or have long-lasting mood changes after listening to the nightly news reports. You may also be driven into a deep melancholy whenever you learn of tragedies around the world.

Personal boundaries are there to protect our emotional lives so that we are not constantly drawn into the drama around us. They define our sense of self and counteract the hidden agenda of wanting to be "liked." They allow others to have their own experiences without us needing to help or fix them or to make them happy.

When you are mistreated in some way, having clear personal boundaries enables you to say, "That is not okay! I am not going to be treated this way" – an adult version of the toddler's insistence on playing with his blocks, *his* way.

Establishing and practicing healthy boundaries begins by first defining them. But what if you do not know how to identify what your personal boundaries should look like? Try observing them in others. We tend to recognize more easily when other people's boundaries have been violated; we react with a sense of outrage or horror. This is a sign of a healthy empathy for others. We may promise ourselves such a thing will never happen to us, but then it does and we end up feeling helpless.

If this happens to you, you may realize your self-empathy may not be as strong as you had hoped, or that your boundaries are not clearly defined. Look at others' boundaries for help with defining your own – but make sure you complete the work of defining your personal boundaries.

I had an experience like the one I just described in seminary during the final meeting for our field education assignment at a nursing home. Our supervisor asked us to share comments about one another as a way of capping off the year. For some reason, one of my classmates said something vague and critical about my ministerial abilities and my way of relating to people. Like lemmings, all the other students around the table followed suit, as if there had been a secret intention to offend me. I was stunned, since none of them had worked alongside me nor knew me well enough to offer *ad hominem* comments. The supervisor, who also ran the seminary field education program, just sat there without commenting. I had wished that someone would have come to my defense. I was livid but swallowed my feelings, fearing I would be criticized for showing anger; in the Boston Catholic ethos priests were never to show even justifiable anger without serious consequences. I realized in this moment that something was wrong; I did not have clearly defined boundaries.

There is a time and place to assist others with their boundary issues. When you have observed another's boundaries being violated, you may have perhaps tried to help, only to get an angry reaction to your attempt. Those of us who have worked with addicts know that they tend to seek help only when they hit their own personal bottom line, which may be very different for each person. The same is true of personal boundaries.

It is important to come to the point of recognizing your boundaries and doing something constructive to help yourself when they are violated rather than relying on sympathy, righteous indignation, resentment, affirmation from authorities, or envy. It is also important to learn to ask for help during moments of violation because most of the people around you will be afraid to "interfere" in a personal matter. Many battered women have learned this lesson the hard way.

I will never forget "Dawn" who came to the church office one day distraught and wanting my help. Dawn had lived with an alcoholic and abusive father. I never found out much about her divorced husband but her current boyfriend "Stan" had just returned after several months in jail for drug possession. He had been emotionally abusive, had drug issues and no job and was living with Dawn and her two teenaged sons. She told me she felt miserable that he was not contributing to the household. "What should I do?" she asked.

"Do you think your life would be better if he weren't living with you?" I asked. "What would it be like if you asked him to leave?"

She listened and protested that she could not just abandon him. I saw her weeks later still emotionally miserable and depressed. And still living with Stan.

Most of us are like Dawn. We tend to address our challenges gradually, as we put one piece at a time into the puzzle of our lives. As much as I wanted to help I knew that Dawn had to recognize, herself, that her boundaries were being violated. Also, I had to be firm about my own boundaries. I had to be willing to let her sit in her misery until she was ready and willing to build a new life.

Many, like Dawn, enjoy talking about their misery, sucking others into their emotional whirlpool and affirming their status as victims. Old habits of thinking and believing as well as old stories that we allow to define us may no longer work for us but we can get stuck in them nonetheless until we get fed up and courageous enough to take the next good step.

Here is a tool to help you know where your personal emotional boundaries begin and end:

Four Steps to Clarifying Boundaries

First, begin with your core values. What are they? Your boundaries usually are based in your core values – the beliefs and qualities we cherish and by which you live. Write in your journal the five to ten beliefs, relationships, activities, or personal qualities about your life that you admire and value the most, that are absolutely necessary for you to live a fulfilling life and that you are willing to die for. Examples are *abundance, affection, bravery, empathy, generosity, enthusiasm, faith, loyalty, professionalism, competence.* If you need help with this refer to corevalueslist.com or mypersonalimprovement.com. Write the ones that resonate with you the most in a column at the left margin of your paper.

Second, for each of the values, describe how it feels for you when it is being respected and affirmed by you and others. Assign a score using a scale of "0-10," with "0" being the most negative feeling possible, "10" being the most positive feeling possible, and "5" as neutral, next to each. So in sum, determine for each value: "When <Value X> is being RESPECTED I feel (0-10)."

Third, describe how it feels when each of these values are violated or disrespected. To the right of the first number, assign a score for each value using the same scale of "0-10," with "0" being the most negative feeling possible, "10" being the most positive feeling possible, and "5"as neutral. Determine for each value: "When <Value X> is being VIOLATED I feel (0-10)."

Fourth, start a new column to the right. Subtract the number you assigned to each value in column 3, when it was VIOLATED or disrespected, from the number you assigned to each value when it was RESPECTED and affirmed. Write these results in the fourth column. Each value will be a score between 0-10.

The values with the highest scores indicate the core values that touch on your most important boundaries. These are the values that are very important for you to uphold in your life. Use them to help you define the boundaries beyond which you do not want to go. Violating your own core values will cause you to feel the most hurt because it is a violation of your personal boundaries. Honoring them will cause you to feel the most elated. Knowing what they are will help you speak up in your own defense. The lowest scored values are neutral or indicate values that are not as central to your life and personal boundaries at this time.

Healthy Boundaries

Healthy boundaries enable us to live each day as people of integrity. We are able to say "yes" and "no" to requests for help without feeling guilty or beholden.

When you know your boundaries, you can examine the physical, social, emotional, intellectual, and spiritual spheres of your lives and determine in what circumstances you feel comfortable or uncomfortable. You can begin to identify which actions or words trigger discomfort and demand you take protective action. Healthy boundaries keep you from giving away your power to anyone. This does not mean you do not help others or ask for help, but it does mean that you draw the line between giving assistance and being used.

Maybe you are already clear about your most important boundaries. Perhaps you have noticed that one or more of them lets in negative energy and you do not do enough to defend it. What can you do to strengthen your boundaries, to address violations, and to shift your beliefs and habits so that your personal boundaries can withstand the daily stresses from the world around us? Try this exercise:

Five Steps to Building Healthier Boundaries

Take your time to breathe throughout this exercise because it can bring up strong emotional reactions. Listen to your breath's inhale and exhale and breathe from your stomach, opening up the muscles from your torso down to your hips.

First, think of a time someone has violated a personal boundary of yours. As you think about it, identify the feeling in your body that comes up. Your body will sense that something is wrong and will transmit the emotional reaction into a physical feeling such as abdominal discomfort, an ache in the neck or head, the gritting of your teeth or an overall feeling of nervousness. Describe the physical sensation and where it shows up in your body. Write down the words that tell about the physical discomfort.

Second, describe the intensity of the sensation using the scale of "0-10" with "0" being no discomfort to "10" being unbearable. Write the number down.

Third, describe how the sensation makes you feel emotionally. Write down the words that describe your feelings, such as scared, nervous, sad, anxious or angry.

Fourth, picture your ideal, strong, intuitive, wise self. See yourself as peaceful and calm. Write down, briefly, the sequence of events that led to your boundaries being violated without judgment or blame. What was said or done by the other person? What did you say or do? What feelings do you remember having at the time?

Fifth, speak your truth now. Say out loud and convincingly: "It was not okay that <X> did/said <Y> to me." Now describe in more detail what was not okay. Write about it in your journal. The below example uses something called the *Reframing and Clarification of Boundaries Model*:

a) It was not okay that Tina made those comments about the way I was dressed. I felt ashamed. My new boundary:

Next time this happens, I will say to Tina, "I'm fine with the way I dress and really do not need your comments unless I ask for them."

b) It was not okay for Fred to criticize me in front of the boss. I felt angry. My new boundary: I will go to Fred in a quiet moment and say "I welcome constructive criticism and I prefer that you would have told me in private. I felt like you were undercutting me in front of the boss."

c) It was not okay for Seth to grab me and try to kiss me. I felt violated. My new boundary: I will tell Seth, "I will choose who will show me affection, what kind, and when. Don't ever do that again."

Conquering the Bully

A major boundary issue that is finally receiving major media attention is that of bullying. The act of bullying affects our boundaries like a one-ton cannon ball shattering the ramparts of a fortress: There is bound to be damage. Ongoing bullying is so disrespectful to our boundaries that our boundaries almost evaporate. Victims of bullying are left with little sense of self and witnesses of the bullying are often left feeling helpless.

Bullying destroys personal defenses with messages of being inadequate, wimpy, cowardly, weak, defective, shameful, ugly or isolated. As with all abuse, the feeling of being bullied lives subjectively in the experience of the one being abused, so we dare not judge when we think someone is or is not being bullied. The victim defines his or her experience and we need to take it at face value. In fact, our denial or doubt that the victim was truly violated is just another form of bullying, leaving the victim feeling even more isolated and shamed.

Those who bully others rarely see themselves in that light, so it is up to their victims and their advocates to call them out. Bullies, whether children or adults, will cloak their abuse as harmless "amusement," as a way to "teach a lesson," or as a means of venting their own anger or frustration. In the past, people used to tolerate bullies as aberrations who came and went; they saw the bully's actions as simply a phase in the bully's development, or as an indication of the bully's maladjustment. As a result, bullying was often minimized. People rarely considered the devastating effect on the victims nor did they recognize the objective truth that bullies destroy lives. More often than not, the bullies themselves were victims of abuse as well. That ought not be an excuse for them, though. No matter what the cause, a bully takes advantage of the sensitivity, fear and ethics of those onto whom they feel they can dump their emotional trash.

Having been bullied myself, I know that we victims can internalize the bullying and end up beating ourselves up in the process. We rehearse the story of being abused over and over and find new ways to be hyper-critical of ourselves. The self-criticism becomes a core value that ratifies our victim status. As a result, we continue to judge ourselves as defective and inadvertently wallow in toxic shame. We find healing only when we expel the demon of the bully from our bodies and souls, so that it no longer has power over us. We then can rebuild our boundaries and ensure that others respect them.

Expelling a bully can be accomplished by creating a ritual. A ritual is a simple exercise that involves our bodies, our breaths, our voices and our emotions in an action that effectively expels the internalized negative energy. Rituals can help physically and symbolically shift the energy within. All they require is a safe and private space.

If you are experiencing bullying, 1 encourage you to get help so you can move beyond it. For more information on creating rituals please contact me or another professional who is familiar with rituals (michael@parisecoaching.com).

Making Sense of Suffering

"Tell your heart that the fear of suffering is worse than the suffering itself. And that no heart has ever suffered when it goes in search of its dreams, because every second of the search is a second's encounter with God and with eternity."

— Paulo Coelho, *The Alchemist*

Suffering, as with all emotions, is neither inherently negative or positive. But there is no doubt that what we humans describe as suffering can be disquieting to our bodies and minds. Some suffering, such as childbirth, usually produces good results, as does the suffering the comes from hard, productive work, athletic training or studying math and science disciplines.

For some of us, a daily inconvenience such as traffic gridlock causes tremendous suffering but there is nothing that can be done about it. When we allow ourselves to undergo this kind of suffering it is usually because we tell ourselves stories that turn us into victims, like: "Traffic delays are unfair! Getting to work isn't supposed to be this hard!" In these moments we ignore the true causes of our suffering: our egos that are telling us that we are supposed to be different from everyone else. We allow ourselves to suffer certain stresses and traumas that upset our nervous and hormonal systems so much that we end up with post-traumatic stress disorder. We can let ourselves suffer a broken heart that even results in illness or death.

We do not always need to focus on the psychological or physical discomfort in suffering. The suffering we experience in any given moment may mask its actual cause.

When you find yourself suffering, it is an indication that there is something you need to reflect on. Suffering may carry with it a message you need to hear. It may point to personal boundaries that need shoring up, to an overblown ego, to codependence, to an unconscious fear, or to hidden narcissism. You can also use your experience of suffering to discover your truest self, to alert you to a value you may not be honoring at that moment or to test the strength of your convictions. Suffering can be a portal to a new life, a new perspective, and new opportunity. Understanding why you are suffering requires that you be brutally honest with yourself. The hardest truth to face may be that much of your personal suffering is self-induced due to living an inauthentic life based in illusory ideals. But although this truth might be the hardest to admit, doing so gives you an immense amount of freedom.

Global Vision and Compassion

Suffering is part of the human condition but that does not stop us from wanting to respond to it in some way. Some of us look at the human experience with a global perspective, taking into account how the many parts of our world interrelate. We may sense the suffering of whole populations and want to do something about it. Others may take a more local viewpoint and focus on our immediate communities and relationships.

One of the reasons I left the parish priesthood was that I had no outlet for my global vision for the church. I felt constrained under leadership whose end-focus was almost always local. Every time a new Archbishop arrived in Boston, I hoped the change would offer an opportunity to share more about my global vision. I dreamed of restructuring the church in a way that would serve all people more effectively, open up communication, and challenge the faithful to shift their perspective away from religious practice for its own sake and toward transformational spiritual relationship.

Global visions can be disquieting. Mine pricked my conscience to such a degree that I simply could no longer acquiesce to the rules of the game established by the system. I had to get out of the suffocating milieu in order to find my voice. The same is true of whistle-blowers, peaceful demonstrators and men and women who have been exiled or imprisoned for daring to speak the truth out loud. The greatest reform movements have almost always been the result of a few people with a global vision who could not be silent in the face of injustice, poverty or conflict.

Ultimately, our view of life, whether global or focused on our immediate environment, ought to *unlock compassion for others*. Compassion, "to suffer with," is at the core of empathy. Compassion is the most radical concept we can embrace in this world of rapid change. It has the power to transform and heal because it is a strong motivator in finding good solutions even amidst the most intractable of problems.

Not all of what we name as compassion is equivalent. Simply feeling sorry for others or having sympathy for their situation does little to help them. The news media do a great job of tugging at our heartstrings by showing interviews after a tragedy or by featuring human interest stories, but some of this hyperbolic reporting serves only to create a distracting empathy-overload that does little to activate true compassion, solve the original problem or help to alleviate unnecessary suffering.

So how do we change lives around us for the better?

Use your empathy, listen to your heart for the cues that lead you to take appropriate action, encourage participation in the solution, refuse to feed the cycle of cynical negativism in social media, and offer shining examples of virtue to inspire others. With the self-awareness of your infinite value, and *compassion for yourself*, you can offer compassion toward even just one other person in some practical, concrete way. This is the start of the transformation toward healing, wholeness, and integration in the world.

FOR REFLECTION:

- What boundary issues do you struggle with most of the time?
- How do you take in other people's emotions and make them your own?
- What action can you take to protect your emotional boundaries, especially from bullies?
- How does compassion motivate your words and actions daily?

Chapter 10

The Power of Empathy

"When we honestly ask ourselves which persons in our lives mean the most to us, we often find that it is those who, instead of giving advice, solutions, or cures, have chosen rather to share our pain and touch our wounds with a warm and tender hand. The friend who can be silent with us in a moment of despair or confusion, who can stay with us in an hour of grief and bereavement, who can tolerate not knowing, not curing, not healing and face with us the reality of our powerlessness – that is a friend who cares."

— Henri J.M. Nouwen, *Out of Solitude: Three Meditations on the Christian Life*

I dislike professional networking events because my deafness and tinnitus prevent me from hearing individuals when more than one person is talking. What I do to survive these events, which often include a yummy lunch, is open my empathic pathways to snare a similarly wired individual and have lunch with them. The other day I met a fascinating and brilliant woman from Australia. We had much in common and had similar temperaments and spirits. She was my lifeline for the day!

Empathy is the part of our human Spirit that is like an open door. It invites connection, intimacy, and companionship into our lives. In turn, empathy offers understanding, help, respect, love and embrace. Nothing makes us more human, and more God-like than empathy.

We had our first experience of empathy in infancy when our parents rushed to our side to comfort, feed, or change our diapers. All we needed to do was whimper. We learned from this first act of love and service that we are meant to depend on one another, to meet one another's needs unconditionally, and to base our friendships on a deep sense of caring. One result of this caring is the deep contentment that we are not living in isolation, that we are not alone.

We know we are being empathic when we send out energy like a fishing net cast into unknown waters. We hope to catch someone's attention because we perceive in our intuition that there is a need to be filled, a relationship that is possible or a soul that needs comforting. In turn, we respond to the empathy from those who are sending out the same kind of energy. We perceive it in their demeanor, their eyes, the tone of their voice, and the content of their speech.

Sometimes we are the ones who take on the role of the helper. We perceive that someone needs us. Other times the role is reversed as someone with a deep empathy reaches out to us in our suffering or time of need. Then there are the beautiful moments when two empaths meet and trade tender care for one another to the benefit of both.

You know empathy is operating when your encounter is not forced or awkward; when it flows naturally and easily as if the relational bond had been there all the time. Sometimes the degree of empathy is so strong that you are able to read the life of the other after only a few questions and you understand profoundly what the other is going through.

What if you are in need of an empathic ear and realize that those around you cannot fill that need? When you are in transition—when change has rocked your foundations, for example when you are in the midst of grief and loss—you need *empathy* and not sympathy. Empathy is the ability to share someone else's feelings. Sympathy is a supportive feeling of sorrow for someone else's troubles. Empathy helps you feel like you are not alone and that you have support in what you are going through. I thank the Universe daily for the wonderful spiritual directors I have known over the years who empathized with my journey and who were good companions in my struggles.

We seek people who will walk through the darkness with us and share in our struggle. That is why I think everyone ought to have a spiritual director or life coach – a trained professional whose business it is to be an empathic listener. You can find just the right one for you by trying them on for size at first and letting your intuition tell you who exhibits the empathic spirit and intelligence you need, rather than merely giving us a sympathetic nodding of the head and sorrowful gaze. You may have a friend or relative who already fulfills that purpose.

Empathy *transforms*. It is like alchemy that changes coal into gold. Genuine empathy can change dark moods into hopefulness. By opening our hearts to what others are suffering, even when we cannot do much about what they are going through, we ratify our common humanity and thus build bridges of intimacy and community.

When you express empathy, you are also able to see through those who seem to "have it made" and who try to mask their suffering. Suffering is easily evident to the empath. By having empathy, you get to know people at their core and you can learn about them from their heart-energy. You build up your wisdom and respect for the complexity of human life.

Empathy ultimately changes human consciousness and brings about global transformation. St. Benedict of Nursia (born circa 480 CE) did not realize it at the time, but his empathic vision for monasticism and community changed the world. He was born into a distinguished Italian family, studied in Rome and later withdrew to a cave high in the mountains for three years. He left behind a depressing world of armies on the march. He empathized with a church torn apart by competing factions and people suffering from war and low morality. He sensed what was needed to restore order and peace and established a rule of life that prescribed a rhythm of liturgical prayer, study, manual labor, living together in community, and compassion for others in need. Soon there was a network of abbeys that each helped Europeans emerge from the dark ages following the fall of the Roman Empire. The abbeys provided order, safety and practical assistance to the poor in the form of agriculture, education and medicine in a time when social safety nets were nonexistent. Benedict's vision built empathy and compassion into the daily workings of the community and became the model for many subsequent religious and civic organizations.

In this chapter I will discuss how deeply embedded empathy is in our every interaction. I begin with the power of empathy in friendship and in forming our personal integrity. I will then speak about being empathic with yourself and steps to becoming your own best friend. I will next address being strong and vulnerable, the power of the human spirit, and discovering new ways to be vulnerable. I will bring empathy full-circle as you get in touch with your wonder-child, the core of who you are. I will end with a method to coach your own soul.

Empathy and Friendship

"I do not ask the wounded person how he feels, I myself become the wounded person."

— Walt Whitman, *Song of Myself*

All empathic encounters lead to friendship on some level. Good spiritual directors and life coaches are not merely trained professionals; they become *friends*. All true friendship begins with a conscious and practical regard for the other.

Why do friendships end then? Because empathy must be nourished by regular contact and conscious desire. Physical distance, lack of heartfelt communication and changes in relationships can get in the way of regular contact. Changes in our lives, both positive and challenging, will also change how we relate to our friends or how they view us. Emotional or spiritual wounding, unresolved hurt, and resentment can sabotage conscious desire to maintain some relationships. We cannot be surprised that we lose friends when we have not taken the steps to maintain contact or when we have been unable to resolve a conflict, especially if the other has cut off communication.

When I left the priesthood, two dear friends cut off communication from me, no matter how I tried to contact them. Their son eventually told me that, "Change is difficult for some people." I still miss them and grieve over the loss of the thirty-year relationships. Yet, friendships do end. Those of us who are particularly empathic feel their endings deeply and need time to let the relationships go. There often is no clean and neat resolution for the dilemma nor are we always able to know all the factors that contributed to the estrangement. So we are forced to live with the resulting ambiguity, and to surrender to the reality with dignity.

What friendships in your life have come to an end? Was it an experience of gradual estrangement for you, or a more dramatic and messy ending? The pain and grief you feel is due to your empathic soul. Paradoxically you know that you are fully alive when you experience pain resulting from your empathy and deep caring for others. I wish there were another way; anything less would diminish being fully human.

Empathy and Integrity

> *"When you are content to be simply yourself and don't compare or compete, everyone will respect you."*
>
> — Lao Tzu, *Tao Te Ching*

Empathy starts with compassionate regard for another and brings together the harmonious working together and co-operation of body, mind and Spirit. This is the definition of *integrity*. Having integrity is an either-or proposition; there is no middle ground. All the empathy we feel and the compassion we sense adds to our personal integrity – our wholeness as *human-beings-in-action*.

Integrity grows with self-awareness. The person with whom we are the cruelest, most heartless and impatient is sometimes ourselves. Why do we give ourselves such a hard time? We may be holding ourselves to a higher standard so that we might be different than those of whom we do not respect. We may imagine others are judging us, even though they do not know us. We may be trying to squeeze our square pegs into round holes, blaming our families of origin for our unhappiness, or justifying ourselves and making excuses. We may be building up resentments based on unreasonable expectations.

If you are doing any of these things, it is due to a lack of self-awareness and integrity. Authentic compassion builds your integrity as you consciously use it to deepen your conviction that you are your own best friend. It enables you to listen to your heart for the cues you need that lead you to the next right step. Compassion has little to do with the warm feeling you get when you help others or receive a positive outcome – it is about having a big enough heart that you dare risk yourself to take the appropriate action in the right moment.

In this journey of self-awareness, the goal is for compassion, motivated by integrity, to become second-nature, moving you to act automatically, without having to calculate how much you may be inconvenienced by taking the action. It has got to be *the right thing to do* for no other reason than your heart says it is the right thing to do, *now*. Compassion allows you to create true community of the heart and to accept each person around you as a unique manifestation of love in action.

Self-empathy

For most of us, it is easier to make friends and have empathic connections and positive regard for others, than it is to make friends with ourselves. We are often our worst critics, withholding empathy as if we are not supposed to receive it from ourselves. But the key here is that, as we develop a true friendship with ourselves, and foster an appreciation—and even humor—about our own foibles and personality quirks, we will be better able to appreciate unusual qualities in others and to extend empathy and compassion to people around us.

So how do you become your own best friend? Here are my steps to support you in this journey:

Six Steps to Becoming Your Own Best Friend

First, know and respect your boundaries. This means you are also aware of your personal emotional landscape. Do you tend to be highly sensitive? Are you more, or less inclined to sense the emotions of others? Are there are topics you cannot discuss with anyone? What are the emotions you most readily express? How do you empathically perceive they get received by others? Do you readily jump into relationships or do you stay on the sidelines waiting for the other to make the first move? Are you clear as to what is and is not okay with you in your interactions with others? Can you tell people if they have crossed your boundaries and that you do not like it?

Second, be grateful. In describing yourself, what are five positive qualities that most people say you have? What do you love about your physical appearance? What aspects of your personality give you joy? What are you really good at doing? Name five of your talents and skills. How do you describe your personal spirituality? How do you show gratitude? The conscious decision to be thankful for what you have and who you are will change your body chemistry, lift your Spirit and shift your attitude, and is the starting point for appreciating yourself as others do.

Third, watch out for the "Victim" and seek the "Sage." A huge internal saboteur is the Victim – the voice inside you that tells you that you are too much to handle, or that you are not enough. The Victim tells you that you have lost out on life's advantages and that you have had a more difficult life than the rest of the human race. Have you met your Sage, your wise, intuitive, self? How does your Sage deal with the Victim? You first need to become familiar with the voice of the wise Sage that is in you. You may be so used to hearing from the Victim that you have overlooked the many ways in which your personal experience and wisdom already expresses itself, especially through the feeling of hope. How has your self-care and advice seen you through rough patches in the past? Are you confident that *you* will help you again, and again?

Fourth, be aware of the "Judge." If you judge others, you are likely to be even harsher on yourself. You may not be aware of why people act as they do and all your intuition tells you is that you do not like it. How do you deal with that insight? What would happen if you became more conscious of what you *do* like about yourself and others, and affirm the wonderful gift you and they are – whole and complete packages, ready to transform the world? Imagine a world without judgment.

Fifth, claim your competence and wholeness. You are talented – in fact you have *genius* that emerges in the way you live, think and complete tasks. You are sufficient and competent. You were also born a complete and whole person who is perfect in this moment. When you look to a relationship to complete you, you are doing yourself a disservice. If you cannot live without someone, especially when that person is harming you in some way, then take responsibility for yourself to protect the child within you. If you need someone or something to make you happy then find out more about codependence and how to recover from it. Seek healing through meditation, counseling or coaching but *do not let yourself get stuck looking for the perfect mate.*

Sixth, consciously seek integrity. The more deeply you send empathic energy into your heart and soul, the readier you will be for a spectrum of healthy friendships and a satisfying career. Integrity lives in bringing together all the parts of life you need to be and enjoying the whole you. Ask, "What about me?" Discover a habit for self-regard and put yourself first in order to achieve the integration you seek.

Strong and Vulnerable

There are many ways to define and describe the concept of *strength*: physical prowess, the ability to survive hardship, emotional fortitude, courage in battle and the power to overcome odds stacked against us. We know where physical strength and stamina come from: exercise, the right attitude and good nutrition. But where does the deeper strength of character and inner courage come from? It comes from being vulnerable.

I have discovered that vulnerability is not weakness. Many times in meetings I will lead with a personal story or a candid question or opinion that reveals what's going on in my mind and heart. In doing so I try to set the tone so that others also have permission to be vulnerable, to speak their truth and to know that they will be listened to with respect.

Vulnerability is not neediness. It is the portal to empathy toward self and others. When we are vulnerable, we come to know who we are through our strengths and during our challenges. It is important for us to know our limits and acknowledge our weaknesses without judgment or condemnation. It is also vital to acknowledge and articulate our inner strengths that sustain us through all adversity.

Vulnerability also has to do with *humility* – knowing we are "of the earth" (human=humus) and that our physical bodies will return to mere dust upon our deaths. When we are vulnerable, we know we are important but not indispensable. We seek to live out our passion in life and we do what we love the most even if we do not do it perfectly. We know that the value is in the *doing*.

Humility keeps you balanced and close to your origins as part of the beautiful and mysterious universe we inhabit. It keeps your thoughts in clear perspective, knowing that likely nothing you perceive, feel, or conceptualize is wasted.

Theologians have called this the "economy of grace," whereby everything in your life is somehow of value to everyone who has ever lived and who has yet to come into physical existence.

Human Spiritual Energy

Our culture has decided that the genders must have clear delineation based on the physical and hormonal differences between men and women. This is very limiting. There is much more to being human than stereotyping gender identity. When we emphasize gender differences we miss the important fact that gender differences are negligible compared with our similarities. Under the skin we are human Spirits, each with a wide range of energetic expression.

Brené Brown in her book, *Daring Greatly* (Penguin Group, NY, 2012) writes about our cultural gender biases:

"When it comes to men, there seem to be two primary responses [to shame]: pissed off or shut down. ...Of course, like women, as men develop shame resilience, this changes, and men learn to respond to shame with awareness, self-compassion, and empathy." (page 96)

She also writes, *"The real struggle for women...is that we're expected...to be perfect, yet we're not allowed to look as if we're working for it. We want it to just materialize somehow. Everything should be effortless. The expectation is to be natural beauties, natural mothers, natural leaders and naturally good parents, and we want to belong naturally. These messages get into our bodies."* (page 87)

Brown's point is that in today's culture, a boy or a man who shows vulnerability is thought to be weak, emotional, un-manly or pathetic. In a similar fashion, a girl or woman who takes the bull by the horns, has strong leadership skills and speaks directly is viewed as a brat, aggressive or manipulative.

Both of these limiting stereotypes have contributed to a lot of unnecessary conflict at home and at work, especially among those who favor a simplistic black and white dualism between the genders. We forget that each gender is capable of the full range of human empathy and vulnerability and that every person has these qualities in varying proportions depending on their circumstances, their experiences, and the fabric of their soul.

All women can be both vulnerable *and* strong, having the tenderness, empathy, and compassion of a mother while also having profound fortitude, decisiveness and the courage of a warrior. There is nothing wrong with viewing women as having both masculine and feminine qualities. Yet our culture often deprives both men and women of possessing the same spectrums of energy. It seems that American men in particular must only be masculine in the narrowest sense of the term. A man who has feminine qualities is often automatically disqualified from the community of "manliness." This prejudice belies how much femininity is entirely misunderstood!

Human spiritual energy is a mix of feminine and masculine energies, both derived from erotic energy, the force behind all creativity. **Feminine** energy nurtures the more vulnerable and holds a safe container for life, for the free expression of emotions and for the development of cooperative relationships on all levels. **She** offers support for compromise, takes a stand when threatened, and nourishes **herself** in order to nourish others.

Masculine energy supports forward movement, builds community spirit, risks all to protect the vulnerable and needy, identifies and achieves goals, delves into adventure and discovery, and seeks ways to implant new life and ideas. **He** fights for justice, defends **himself** and **his** mates, and gives **himself** totally when called upon.

Now switch the bolded words in the previous two paragraphs: *masculine* for *feminine*, *he* for *she* and *himself* for *herself*. Do you notice how both paragraphs actually describe either gender?

The genders have been consciously rebalancing masculine and feminine energy in our world for the past hundred years as we have moved through embracing women's participation in public policy, industry, science, and social welfare more fully than before. Still, much more has to be done, but we have come a long way. We are also more deeply appreciating the gifts that gay and lesbian people manifest in their unique combinations of masculine and feminine spiritual energies. We are seeing an irrevocable trend throughout the world (and its backlash) that accepts being lesbian, gay, bisexual, or transgender as having always been vital to the human spirit. The particular spiritual gifts of LGBTQ folk have enriched society in countless ways and can serve as necessary counterpoints to the hypermasculine and hyperfeminine stereotypes that have limited the fullest expression of humanity in the past.

Discovering Vulnerability

A central theme of Jesus' life was allowing vulnerability to live on the surface. He permitted others to witness his weaknesses and the ambiguities of his life. He also avoided labeling, judgment, a narrow interpretation of cultural norms and both offensive and defensive posturing. Jesus let his vulnerability be his strength – a mirror in which others could see themselves without qualification, justification or self-pity. There is a quote from one of St. Paul's letters that remains a classic reminder of the origins of true strength:

> "For this thing I asked the Lord three times, that it might depart from me. And he said to me, 'My grace is sufficient for you: for my strength is made perfect in weakness.' Most gladly therefore will I rather glory in my infirmities, that the power of Christ may rest upon me. Therefore, I take pleasure in infirmities, in reproaches, in necessities, in persecutions, in distresses for Christ's sake: for when I am weak, then am I strong." (II Corinthians 12:8-10)

Whatever was plaguing Paul at the time, it is clear that it brought him to his knees. Once an active persecutor of Jesus' followers, he now confronted his vulnerability and powerlessness. In surrendering, he found his true strength through his newfound spiritual awakening. Like Mahatma Gandhi, Martin Luther King, and others in the great tradition of non-violent resistance to oppression, whenever we capitalize on our vulnerability we let loose the best of our masculine and feminine energies. In vulnerability something greater than the sum of the parts manifests itself as a witness to true strength and surrender simultaneously.

Where do we discover the value in our vulnerability? Usually it begins in our family of origin. The imprinting from our parents and guardians as to how they dealt with, or denied, emotion, is so powerful that, short of a military-style retraining program, brainwashing program, or a trauma, it remains fixed in stone. We always carry a bit of our previous generations deep within our souls.

Parents sometimes forget how powerful their example of teaching empathy through their own vulnerability is. Fathers enjoy a unique bond with their children. They usually do not use words to show their vulnerability; they simply act on it. The deeper meaning behind their actions gets communicated, yet often remain hidden from view. Fathers and men show strength through vulnerability in their own unique masculine ways and this can help to complete the picture children need for their own growth in emotional vulnerability. This can lead children to be more open to loving and healthy relationships. The following is a short list of the ways masculine strength and vulnerability shines through which I gleaned from my collective experience of different fathers I have met:

Learning to be in their bodies. Men tend to be more physical in expressing their energy. Children learn to become more comfortable with how their bodies support them through their fathers' active presence.

A sense of adventure, wonder and awe. Men have a unique way of opening up the world as a place of wonder and awe; of new experiences and heroic challenges. The "inner child" in most men loves to go out to enjoy such adventures.

Relational stability. A mother's instinct is so strong that she will almost never abandon her children. A father shows that he has made a deliberate and conscious choice to support and nurture his family.

Unconditional acceptance. A father's hopes for his children complement a mother's. Children need to feel encouragement and support from their fathers as they fulfill their destinies. Children who perceive themselves as measuring up in their father's eyes carry this glowing image throughout their lives.

Masculine love. Masculine love tends to dominate in men as feminine love does in women. Fathers possess and express both the protective and nurturing aspects of love, modeling them in a unique way to teach self-acceptance and respect.

Learning how to be safe. Fathers teach their children how to defend themselves in an ethical manner and how to win an argument by exercising self-respect and self-control.

Respecting the opposite sex. Boys and girls need male examples to help them develop healthy relationships with the opposite sex, appropriate sexual and personal boundaries and self-regard.

Modeling fair play, ethical standards, and honesty in communication. A father's perspective in dealing with teams, jobs, friendships, and projects is a necessary counterpoint to that modeled by mothers.

Masculine spirituality. Relating to the transcendent, a man shows children how to relate fully and deeply to the universal Spirit and how to develop both the vulnerable and brutally honest aspects of relating to God.

Sustaining family. Men teach children how to love others through his loving of their mother. This relationship models appropriate masculine/feminine bonding and unconditional sacrifice. Children who see how their fathers take initiative and responsibility to make their mother's life easier are much happier. In addition, when children also know that their parents are there for them in service to their needs, they are free to seek their own way and find their truest and unique selves.

The Wonder Child

About twenty-five years ago, when I was on my yearly silent eight-day retreat I experienced a profound and mystical interruption that shifted my life forever. On the first day, I was sitting on the rocks of Eastern Point in Gloucester, soaking in the sun and listening to the waves crashing around me. I began reflecting on recent conversations I had been having with God about my "wonder child" – my ideal inner self about whom I had been reading. Suddenly my heart told me to pause and look up. The clouds seemed to part. I saw a child walking toward me with his arms outstretched. I felt him move closer and closer until I felt him enter my soul. I was overtaken by awe; I felt completed; my eyes filled with tears and I wept for hours. I later shared my experience with my retreat director who understood the mystical nature of my experience. I had been reunited with my core identity; with the perfect spiritual child I had always been and as God had always known me.

We all have a wonder child living within us. It is our truest selves – how we were first conceived. As an adult, we can access that child, for our souls have not changed, only our bodies and minds. By listening to and parenting our inner children, we can make up for the shortcomings of our parents. We can open our vulnerable hearts to hold our child-selves close and safe. We can invite our inner children to be part of our present lives – so they are no longer simply past memories.

The reality of our inner children makes sense because we are Spirits living in physical bodies for as long as our lifespans on earth are. Our spirits remain after death – pure Spirits of wonder and awe; Spirits of pure love that have consciousness and who continue to exist in the universe as part of the consciousness of all humanity that ever existed.

Our inner children seek our adult attention, need to be acknowledged and want our adult love. We so often grow up thinking we have left behind our past, when in reality *we are our past, present, and future,* here and now. When we feel out of balance emotionally, or needy, lonely, or empty it is actually that child yearning for our attention. This is another indication that we are being called to self-care and the compassionate recognition of our need for our own attention.

Sometimes we try to ignore the child. We think our adult selves alone have to solve all problems. Yet our inner children have great insights and our real problem is a lack of integration with them on the deepest spiritual level of intimacy.

You can extend yourself to reach out to your younger self and experience how he or she is feeling in real time. The vantage point of adulthood enables you to access your wisdom with your child's pure heart. You also can have a dialogue with your child. You first have to invite the child to be a part of your adult consciousness. Placing your hand on our heart, you can ask the child what needs to be said and listen to what the child says to your adult self through your soul. You can assure the child of your love and protection and that you will not abandon the child again. He or she is merely looking for nurturing from us. You can sit with your child, imagining his or her presence in the room with you and hearing the small voice of your dearest self who is offering you deep truth rooted in love. You hear what the child wishes to say deep in your soul, communicating in a way your parents never could.

What is the soul? The soul is not a thing or an entity. We cannot measure it or weigh it. We cannot even feel it or perceive it with our five primary senses.

You can sense your soul when you consciously perceive yourself in the abstract, viewing yourself in your mind's eye from a distance. It is in that moment when you realize that you are alive and real; when you sense what it means to *be* in this moment.

The soul is also the seat of your consciousness and identity and where your inner child lives. Your soul holds your capacity to love, to relate, emote, intuit, transcend yourself, connect with the infinite and feel part of the wider universe. Your soul's expression reaches its zenith whenever you engage in authentic social, spiritual or sexual intercourse with all of your faculties.

Your soul transcends empirical knowledge and leads you to insight and discernment. God does not live in the soul; rather the soul *is* God. You are suffused with God-energy that flows freely through the universe in the form of conscious, deliberate, and unconditional love. When you hear your soul speaking to you, you simultaneously align the myriad of emotions and sensations your body, mind, and heart are experiencing in that moment.

Coaching the Soul

In *The Practice of Spiritual Direction* (Harper-Collins, 1982), William A. Barry and William J. Connelly write:

> "Spiritual direction is concerned with helping a person directly with his or her relationship with God. ... The ministering person helps the other to address God directly and to listen to what God has to communicate. The focus of this kind of spiritual direction is the relationship itself between God and the person. The person is helped not so much to understand that relationship better, but to engage in it [and] to enter into dialogue with God. Spiritual direction of this kind focuses on what happens when a person listens to and responds to a self-communicating God." (pp. 5-7)

Spiritual direction helps to put us in contact with our soul – coaching our soul, if you will. With the help of a spiritual director, we can align our minds with our hearts. This will help us discern what decisions we need to make based on our deepest desires. This alignment puts into action the full power of self-awareness and promotes congruence between our spiritual and physical life.

A good spiritual mentor will not tell you what to do and will rarely offer advice. Rather, he or she will walk alongside you as a spiritual companion. He or she may come out of a particular spiritual or religious tradition but will not impose this in their relationship with you. Instead they join together with you on an equal footing, walking the journey with you no matter where it takes them. It is a relationship free of judgment, labeling, and preconceptions about God. In this way, you have access to a full range of possibilities and allow your Spirit to move accordingly.

When you coach your soul, you access the full range of your faculties – spiritual, mental, and emotional. Let us use the metaphor of an automobile vacation trip: Your mind gets out the map and determines the direction to follow to your destination. Your heart tells you where you want to stop along the way to fulfill your desires. It is your *soul* that lets you know if this trip is even right for you – if you can afford it, if it is the right time to take it, if you might enjoy it and if it will add value to your life. Your soul holds the overall meaning of the event as its top priority – the reason you embarked on the trip in the first place and how it fits with the overall goals you hope to achieve.

While I would recommend it is best to enter into a relationship with a spiritual mentor or life coach trained in spiritual matters to coach your soul, you can also coach your own soul to ready you for the next good thing that will flow out of your life purpose. Here are some steps on how to do this:

Five Steps to Coaching the Soul

Go to a place where you can be quiet and meditative. Get into a posture that is comfortable for you, without getting so relaxed that you are liable to fall asleep!

First, identify where your soul manifests itself in your body. The soul does not take up space, but there is a spiritual energetic center that self-identifies in each of us. For most of us it is the area of the heart. Place the palm of your hand in that location and keep it there throughout this exercise. This touch creates an energy circuit that calms the body's nervous system.

When you sense the presence of your soul, you may feel a warm, tingling sensation or a sense of relaxation and peace. Be aware of distracting mind chatter and begin to let go of it. Let go also of thoughts that begin with "If only...," I should..." or "I regret..." and other language that keeps you from being in the present.

Second, breathe. Dismiss all thoughts without prejudice. Your breath is the threshold to your soul. Consciously breathe in slowly through your nose and out through your mouth. Let your abdomen expand at your inhale, counting slowly to four. At the peak of your breath, hold it for a two count. Slowly and gently exhale through your mouth for a four count. Repeat this throughout the exercise. If you become distracted, just go back to the breathing – in and out.

Third, after a few centering breaths, become conscious of your hand over your soul. Your eyes should be either closed or softly focused on a lit candle, a sacred image, or a view of nature.

Now it is time for a conversation with your soul. It is time for candor, honesty, plain speech, non-judgment, and clarity.

Fourth, tell your soul how you feel in this moment. Be honest and direct and do not hold back. Just say quietly what your intuition is telling you. Ask your soul, "What do you want to tell me?" and then wait in silence. Wait to hear an inner voice. The soul will always say something that is not only true but also supportive, safe, beautiful, loving and nourishing: "All will be well." "You are enough." "I love you." "You are powerful." "You are strong." "There is nothing to fear." "I will never leave you." "You are wonderful." You will feel the words of your soul even more than you hear them.

Your intuitive heart will feel contentment. You may feel tingling up and down your spine.

Fifth, bathe in what your soul is saying. Bring to your soul your intentions, questions, decisions, and anything on your mind and in your heart that needs clarification. Wait for answers from your soul now or at a later session. When you feel complete, open your eyes and focus on something around you. Then, in your journal, record what your soul shared with you. Bring your mind and heart into the conversation. Ask yourself questions such as: *What is the message of my soul in this moment? What changes in attitude, behavior, or relationships do I need to make? What would my life be like if I were conscious of this message each day? What deep desire has emerged from my heart? What is the impact of this message on my life purpose? What is this message revealing about the direction of my life?*

FOR REFLECTION:

- Who are the people in your life have been were great examples of empathy and service?
- For what are you grateful about yourself?
- How do your masculine and feminine energies manifest in a positive way?
- How are your vulnerabilities actually your greatest strengths?
- What might happen if you focus on your gifts and strengths rather than your imagined inadequacies?

Conclusion

Watch your thoughts; they become words.
Watch your words; they become actions.
Watch your actions; they become habits.
Watch your habits; they become character.
Watch your character; it becomes your destiny.
                                                    —Lao-Tze

This is really not the end but the beginning. You will find it helpful to refer back to various portions of this guide to take charge of your life when everything seems to be changing. I hope that if you have been busy rescuing others, either by choice or circumstance, that you will now give yourself the right to reclaim responsibility over your own life and not relinquish your spiritual health to other people.

Your intuition is your greatest gift. Listening to your heart and gut will always offer clues as to where and how to proceed in life. But as you have learned now, you also need an imperative—a foundation on which to build—to propel you in the direction that will be most life-giving for you. We examined first imperatives together and you looked at ridding yourself of previous first imperatives that no longer serve you as a mature seeker. This process should never stop. Keep looking at your first imperatives to see which continue to serve you, which you need to discard, and which new ones you need to create.

As you discovered in this book, intuition also tells you to seek intimacy on many levels – honest and clean intimacy that is cleansed of old stories, limiting beliefs and resentments. Remember, you may even need to find the courage to examine and redefine the way you have been relating to God as the focus for your transcendent connections. You will continually find that a relationship with God is most helpful when you are brutally honest in what you say and how you say it, when you blurt out your deepest desires and when you refused to be hemmed in by external dogmas that serve no purpose in themselves. Remember that religious or spiritual institutions serve you no spiritual purpose unless they give you the freedom to make decisions based in your deepest conscience.

No matter how you move forward with the life you are meant to be living, you are still going to experience some loneliness, fear, and other challenging emotions that threaten to subvert your best intentions. Keep in mind as you go that making friends with difficult emotions gives you new insight into who you are becoming. They are portals for your transformation and courage.

As you continue to discern the deep desires of your heart you will receive clues as to your true intentions and what you really want. Your heart will tell you whether or not what you are doing is a match who you are in this moment. For example, listen to what your heart says about what you have chosen for a career or job. As you plan and recreate your life, you learn to live in the now where your soul's voice can best be heard. The more you practice this, you will grow to no longer fear change but actually embrace it.

Creating and maintaining healthy personal boundaries as you go through internal changes and as changes occur around you will help you deepen your personal integrity. The parts of your life that change can then dovetail smoothly into the whole. You can continue to grow and serve others by placing yourself in their shoes, sensing their energy and responding in the most helpful ways you can think of, sometimes even doing nothing until they come to the realization on their own that they need to help themselves. You can stay on course by coaching your soul, listening to your heart and taking each step, one at a time, toward wholeness.

If you have read and pondered something in this book that has given you pause, let it change you. Let yourself be challenged by the unknown, the ambiguous and the grey areas that cause you to feel on edge or without a mooring. This signals the edge of *growth* – not of an abyss. Your lack of a mooring will be soon remedied by your Sage who has the rudder of your ship firmly in hand!

The tendency in the Western religions to offer easy answers concerning the future is challenged at every turn if you are engaged in real, inner, personal growth. If you keep going on this journey, you will discover that even God expects you to have no absolute or clear answers to life. The best thing you can do is keep responding in the moment with full awareness and the faith that the answers will come when you are ready to receive them.

Make the intention now to write the conclusion of this book through the expression and quality of your love and service. Make each breath, each thought, and each act your answer to the most important questions: *What about me? How have I moved a step closer to compassion for our Universe, empathy for all creation and ultimate respect for myself? Did I trust Love enough to let Love in, and then did I give Love away, with abandon?*

Appendix

(Published in the *National Catholic Reporter*
as the cover story, June, 2006)

Betraying the tender ideal of the Church

Priests suffer because of the sex abuse scandal

By MICHAEL PARISE

The recent clergy sexual abuse scandal in the Catholic church has revealed an unplanned but ongoing and long-term miscarriage of justice. If we accept the theological dictum, "justice precedes love," it is clear that thousands of Catholic youngsters and their families have been deprived of the church's most basic love, and therefore justice, for decades.

While children are the primary victims of the scandal, the secondary victims are the 95 percent of parish priests who, though innocent of wrongdoing, have been deeply and negatively affected by the past handling of clergy sexual abuse and its present ramifications. It is this group I want to write about.

Many priests have suffered in the depths of their souls as dozens of young people have revealed their horror stories. We have felt degraded as our brother priests have been removed from active ministry. We have been demoralized to see how our bishops had not given basic justice to victims and covered up their allegations with legalism. For many priests, the final coup de grâce was when we had to witness our spiritual fathers, the bishops, formulate policies in Dallas that were designed to protect child-victims but made victims of entire presbyterates.

Nearly 30 years ago in the seminary, I knew of the horrible effects of sexual abuse of minors as a true clinical and pastoral issue. I have spent the last two years asking myself a lot of questions. Why were so many bishops apparently ignorant of the facts behind sexual abuse of children? Why did dioceses keep secret files on their priests and then not refer to them when necessary? How do I reconcile this betrayal of the innocents by their shepherds with my ministry and even with my faith?

A pious-sounding response to these questions would be that bishops and diocesan officials are merely men and prone to the same kinds of weakness and sinfulness as anyone else. After all, this response would continue, many people in our culture had downgraded the importance of sexual abuse of children until relatively recently. Indeed, the incidence of unreported incest in families is epidemic if we are to believe current statistics.

A practical-sounding response to my questions would probably be rooted in the desire to preserve the laity from believing that their clergy are just as prone as anyone else to being scoundrels. The fear of scandal was, and often continues to be, a powerful motivation for the lack of transparency among professional church people.

The concern to buoy the public image of the Catholic church at almost any cost is especially powerful in the United States, where for centuries bishops felt they had to prove their immigrant Catholic population was just as "American" and upstanding as the descendants of the founding fathers. For many decades, Catholics had to deal with a deeply rooted prejudice about the "iniquities" of Catholicism seen through the eyes of non-Catholics.

In addition, clergy sex abuse pressed many hot button issues such as the identity of the priest as an icon of Jesus Christ himself, and not merely as a "minister"; priestly celibacy, viewed as "mystical" at best and "unfair" and "abnormal" at worst; and human sexuality, held hostage by a long-standing dualism between spirit and flesh among Catholics -- exemplified by Jansenism in Irish, French, and Italian immigrant cultures.

Innocent children were almost the only group in scripture whom Jesus protected with severe pronouncements of judgment and punishment for any who harmed them. Tragically, to hide the scandal of clergy sex abuse, justice was withheld from those who needed it most.

Bureaucratic miscarriage

This miscarriage of justice, however, has given birth to another miscarriage of what I call the tender ideal of the church that has motivated priests for centuries. It was this tender ideal of the church that prompted me to change career directions in college and to enter the seminary. Now I know on several levels what it must be like for couples to experience the miscarriage of a much wanted, deeply loved unborn child.

The tender ideal of the church, which God originally planted within my heart, has taken many hits over the last quarter century. Indeed, I would go so far as to say that the greatest challenges I have faced in my priesthood have come from the bureaucratic handling of lay and clergy by the church's institutions. This institutional response is focused on any issue or person that appears to threaten the smooth running of the bureaucracy. It is this *modus operando* that was used to deal with clergy sexual misconduct with children.

I have had a number of personal experiences with this methodology. The one that stands out the most occurred about a decade ago. After leaving a particularly dysfunctional parish assignment, I fell into a deep sadness out of which I was having difficulty emerging. Friends in the priesthood suggested I speak directly to my ordinary, insisting that he would certainly want to know about my situation. I made an appointment and explained to him my disappointment and inability to find a good use for my gifts in parish ministry.

What shocked me at the time, but now makes sense in light of recent revelations of how abuse victims were treated, was his terribly bureaucratic response to my personal concerns. He simply threw the problem back onto me, placing the blame squarely on me. He did not listen to me as a unique individual; he did not validate me or my ministry; he deprived me of any sense of personal credibility. In short, I was a problem to be solved in the most expeditious manner possible. I left the meeting in a state of shock, feeling absolutely worthless.

This experience added to the process of my miscarrying my tender ideal of the church. I am dismayed that other priests have felt dehumanized by the behavior of their ordinaries and diocesan officials, who have viewed them as issues to be managed and not people to be nurtured. I can't help but believe that the crisis of sexual abuse might have been mitigated had more bishops done what I consider to be their primary job: the personal shepherding of their priests as individual and unique gifts to the church, and not as a collective work force. God gives those called to ministry a deep sense of what the church ought to be.

This tender ideal is a feeling of devotion and love for the people of God, and yes, even for the church's institutions and teachings. This ideal motivates a priest daily; it is a source of joy, helping him to share his faith with others. A very useful ideal, it is also very delicate.

Each priest's tender ideal of the church matures with time, according to his personality and experience. It is my hope that the ideal becomes increasingly rooted in reality. Therapists call this process "becoming de-illusioned," rather than disillusioned and therefore cynical. Yet at the core remains this tender embryo of the idea of the church, meant to grow in the priest's heart by the grace of God.

Even in the best of times, this tender ideal receives its share of battering throughout a priest's life. Parishioners often project their anger and disappointment upon their pastors, whom they think have Teflon emotions. Fellow clerics will occasionally use tired political ploys to manipulate one another. Too many bishops, "golden boys" since their seminary days, are unrealistic about the nature of parish ministry and do not treat their priests as friends and collaborators.

It takes a lot of prayer and fortitude as well as a great deal of care to maintain the tender ideal of the church within a priest's vocation. It is his heart, this tender ideal. It embodies his love for God and his quiet passion for God's people. It is something only another priest or religious can fully comprehend.

Yet the tender ideal of the church is not limited to the ordained. It is also found within the laity. It resides in the hearts of all who love Jesus and the church, most especially those innocent among us, who are more freely open to God's grace: our children. Imagine how that ideal has been weakened, and even destroyed, by the church's failure in these recent scandals to carry out the most basic aspect of its mission: to value each person, child or adult, lay or ordained, as infinitely precious and valued in God's sight.

From covenant to corporation

The appalling episcopal response to clergy sexual abuse throughout the decades is a case study of the true evil of bureaucracy in the church. When the church stops being "family" and defaults into a "corporation" model, it loses its identity altogether. It breaks its covenant with God and with God's people. While I have never experienced the horror of being sexually abused as a child, I can understand clearly the pain and anguish that results from not being listened to. Even two years after the scandal broke, many priests continue to feel as if the child we have been carrying since ordination remains stillborn.

The grief I feel is deep and pervasive. The feeling of betrayal is all too real. As I speak with fellow clergy, they tell me that they are in an emotional limbo; they are merely going through the motions of ministry. No one has adequately addressed this grief, or even acknowledged it. I have not heard one bishop make a clear public apology to his priests for the collective mistakes made by the American episcopate and their effect on our ministries.

Unfortunately, the bishops only exacerbated the effects of this miscarriage by their response to the scandal at their meeting in Dallas. In their headlong desire to control damage and undo the wrongs of the past, they further alienated their priests with their rhetoric and their policies. One bishop publicly made patently inaccurate doctrinal statements about the nature of the priesthood. Most seemed to ignore the fact that their priests were even worthy of pastoral consideration. The message in Dallas regarding the accused seemed to be, "Cut them off, cut them out, get rid of them as soon as possible, and protect our episcopal prerogatives! And, oh yes, let's start protecting children from priests from now on!"

To their credit, the response of religious superiors at their own meeting on the same issue was far different. They acknowledged the need to keep criminal clergy away from people but recognized that they were part of a family, and could not be jettisoned at will for the sake of appearances. Someone had to take responsibility for their well-being.

Episcopal abdication

Parish priests have by and large looked to their bishops as spiritual fathers and brothers. This has been central to their tender ideal of the church. Thus, it was particularly painful to us that a large number of bishops seemed to be entirely cut off from the reality of what was happening in their own dioceses. The dynamics of the Dallas meeting, the blanket indictment of homosexual clergy as the cause of the problem, the slow resolution of cases of past allegations, and the lack of support for priests in ministry during this time has driven a mighty wedge between bishops and their priests, a wedge that no amount of pleading, no number of programs, meetings, pious appeals for "unity" and "fraternal support" will heal.

It is a true sign of the power of God that despite the feeling that something precious has miscarried, the majority of priests are still at their posts. Perhaps the reason is they cannot afford to leave (in my diocese there is no vested pension plan for priests; a stipend is paid only to priests who retire in good standing; when a priest leaves, he leaves with almost nothing). Perhaps younger priests are sustained in the hope that the church will continue to change in positive ways. Whatever the motivation for parish priests to continue in their daily grind, I would like to believe that at least there is room for God to work. God truly understands the grief, loss and pain that priests are feeling. God understands our isolation, our lack of support, and our lack of understanding.

God also understands the situation in which the bishops find themselves. Their pain must be similar to ours. Some must feel trapped by the sheer magnitude of their dioceses, whose size is maintained for prestige but not for practicality in governance and pastoral care.

I also believe God permitted this scandal to unfold because no one in power in the church was willing or able to open "Pandora's Box." God has ultimate and perfect justice and compassion for all of us who have been victimized. If we change the way we do business as a community of faith, God can and will revivify that tender ideal of the church now dormant in the souls of many priests, and maybe even of the bishops, too.

About the Author

Michael Parise served as a parish priest in Catholic parishes
around Boston for over 32 years.
He is currently a teacher, mentor, healer, author, and artist. As
the *Life & Spirit Coach*, he is certified in spiritual direction and
emotional recovery. Michael
Parise works in person and by

phone from works from his home in Tampa, Flor-
ida. Michael specializes in helping busy executives
and professionals drowning in responsibilities at
home and work. His integrated and holistic approach to working with the body, mind, and spirit
helps his clients focus on their priorities and sim-
plify their lives so they have more balance and joy.

He offers all readers who are ready to change
a complimentary coaching session. Contact Michael at michael@parisecoaching.com.

Follow his "No More Overwhelm" blog at
www.parisecoaching.com and his Life & Spirit
Facebook page.